MW00355788

Modern Asset Allocation for Wealth Management

Founded in 1807, John Wiley & Sons is the oldest independent publishing company in the United States. With offices in North America, Europe, Australia, and Asia, Wiley is globally committed to developing and marketing print and electronic products and services for our customers' professional and personal knowledge and understanding.

The Wiley Finance series contains books written specifically for finance and investment professionals, as well as sophisticated individual investors and their financial advisors. Book topics range from portfolio management to e-commerce, risk management, financial engineering, valuation, and financial instrument analysis, as well as much more.

For a list of available titles, visit our Website at www.WileyFinance.com.

Modern Asset Allocation for Wealth Management

DAVID M. BERNS, PhD

WILEY

Published by John Wiley & Sons, Inc., Hoboken, New Jersey.
Published simultaneously in Canada.

For general information on our other products and services or for technical support, please contact our Customer Care Department within the United States at (800) 762-2974, outside the United States at (317) 572-3993, or fax (317) 572-4002.

Wiley publishes in a variety of print and electronic formats and by print-on-demand. Some material included with standard print versions of this book may not be included in e-books or in print-on-demand. If this book refers to media such as a CD or DVD that is not included in the version you purchased, you may download this material at http://booksupport.wiley.com. For more information about Wiley products, visit www.wiley.com.

Library of Congress Cataloging-in-Publication Data is Available:

9781119566946 (Hardback)
9781119567004 (ePDF)
9781119566977 (epub)

Cover Design: Wiley
Cover Image: © oxygen/Getty Images

Printed in the United States of America

V10018173_032420

Table of Contents

Preface

Modern portfolio theory (MPT) is one of the most insightful tools of modern finance. It introduced the world to the first intuitive framework for portfolio risk and how one can optimally combine investable assets to form portfolios with high return and low volatility. The elegance and power of mean-variance (M-V) optimization garnered its inventor Harry Markowitz a well-deserved Nobel Memorial Prize in Economics and has always been a great personal inspiration for how quantitative insights can assist us all in our daily life.

The actual process of implementing MPT for clients can be challenging in practice, though. Setting client risk preferences, accounting for client financial goals, deciding which assets to include in the portfolio mix, forecasting future asset performance, and running an optimization routine all sound simple enough conceptually, but when you actually sit down to implement these tasks, the true complexity of the problem becomes apparent. This implementation hurdle forces many advisors either to outsource the asset allocation component of their process or deploy simple portfolio construction heuristics (rules of thumb) that are sub-optimal and lack connection to client preferences.

The financial ecosystem has also seen tremendous evolution since MPT was first introduced in 1952. The world has been introduced to non-linear investable assets such as options and certain alternative risk premia (AKA style premia, factor investing, or smart beta), which have rapidly become more available to retail investors over the past two decades. Additionally, our understanding of human behavior when it comes to decision-making under uncertainly has markedly shifted with the discovery of prospect theory (PT) in the 1970s. *Homo economicus*, the perfectly rational investor, is no longer the client we are building portfolios for. These evolutions cannot be handled in the MPT framework: non-linear assets cannot be represented by mean and variance and the M-V approach cannot capture the nuances of behavioral risk preferences.

While MPT is both practically challenging and theoretically antiquated, there are wonderful new methods available for both simplifying the challenging tasks in the asset allocation process and addressing the realities of human decision-making in today's markets. Unfortunately, this progress has not been widely assimilated by the wealth management community, which includes both traditional advisors and robo-advisors. Most advisors still utilize the original formulation of MPT or deploy heuristic models that help avoid the challenges of implementation altogether. This book is a first step to bridging the gap between the original formulation of MPT and a more modern and practical asset allocation framework.

This book was written to enable advisors to more accurately design portfolios for real-world client preferences while conquering the complexities of the asset allocation process that often push advisors into sub-optimal heuristics or outsourcing. To empower advisors fully in being able to implement the framework catalogued in this book, the complete machinery is available as a cloud-based SaaS: www.portfoliodesigner.com. Just as the book is meant to provide a modern and intuitive system for creating portfolios, the software is also intended to provide an accurate and scalable solution for real-world asset allocation based on the methods presented here. And for those who don't want to deploy the primary framework of the book, the hope is that the materials presented here can minimally help advisors navigate the wide world of asset allocation solutions out there in a more informed and fiduciary manner.

While a primary goal of this writing is to provide a practical solution to asset allocation, I must warn you that the final framework falls short of being a simple solution. Any asset allocation solution that truly respects client preferences and the foundations of modern financial economics will require a certain foundation of knowledge and measured care for proper implementation. My hope is that, with education and practice, the refined perspective presented here will quickly become second nature to wealth management practitioners and ultimately lead to a scalable process that financial advisors can truly stand behind. To help streamline this education, I have decided not to present an encyclopedic review of asset allocation tools, but instead to focus on a limited number of tools for each step of the asset allocation process. To this end, I have consciously focused on the most accurate methods that were simultaneously practical, which includes elements that are undeniably optimal (and need never be replaced) and others that are clearly not optimal (and may warrant replacement). While the ultimately singular framework presented here indeed has its limitations, my truest intention was to create a modern yet practical process that the wealth management community could readily and confidently deploy today.

For the purposes of this book, asset allocation is defined as anything related to creating an investment portfolio from scratch. This includes setting client risk preferences, deciding which assets to include in client portfolios, forecasting future asset performance, and blending assets together to form optimal client portfolios. Following the first chapter, which reviews some key preliminary concepts and presents the general framework pursued here, this book is organized in the order in which each asset allocation task is carried out when creating a client's portfolio in practice. Hence, Chapters 2–5 are meant to serve as a step-by-step guidebook to asset allocation, where the aforementioned software follows the exact same workflow. Below is a brief overview of what will be covered in each chapter.

Chapter 1. Preliminaries. Utility theory and estimation error, two key concepts that underlie much of the book's discussions, are introduced. Asset allocation is then defined as the maximization of expected utility while minimizing the effects of estimation error, which will ultimately lead to the book's modern yet practical process for building portfolios. MPT and other popular models are shown to be approximations to the full problem we would like to solve. Key concepts from behavioral economics are also introduced, including a modern utility function with three (not one) risk parameters, that can capture real-world client preferences. We then review how to minimize estimation error and its consequences to create a practical framework that advisors can actually implement. The chapter ends with a formal definition of the overall framework that is pursued in the remainder of the book.

Chapter 2. The Client Risk Profile. The chapter begins with a review of how to measure the three dimensions of client risk preferences (risk aversion, loss aversion, and reflection) via three lottery-based questionnaires. The concept of standard of living risk (SLR) is introduced to help determine whether these preferences should be moderated to achieve the long-term cash flow goals of the portfolio. SLR is then formally assessed with a comprehensive yet simple balance sheet model, which goes far beyond the generic lifecycle investing input of time to retirement, and leads to a personalized glidepath with a strong focus on risk management. The final output of the chapter is a systematic and precise definition of a client's utility function that simultaneously accounts for all three dimensions of risk preferences and all financial goals.

Chapter 3. Asset Selection. The third chapter presents a systematic approach to selecting assets for the portfolio that are simultaneously accretive to a client's utility and minimally sensitive to estimation error. By combining this asset selection process with the concept of risk premia, the chapter also introduces a new paradigm for an asset class taxonomy, allowing advisors to deploy a new minimal set of well-motivated asset classes that is both complete and robust to estimation error sensitivity.

Chapter 4. Capital Market Assumptions. This chapter justifies the use of historical return distributions as the starting point for asset class forecasts. We review techniques that help diagnose whether history indeed repeats itself and whether our historical data is sufficient to estimate accurately the properties of the markets we want to invest in. A system is then introduced for modifying history-based forecasts by shifting and scaling the distributions, allowing advisors to account for custom forecasts, manager alpha, manager fees, and the effects of taxes in their capital market assumptions.

Chapter 5. Portfolio Optimization. In the fifth and final chapter, we finally maximize our new three-dimensional utility function over the assets selected and capital market assumptions created in the previous chapters. Optimizer results are presented as a function of our three utility function parameters, showcasing an intuitive evolution of portfolios as we navigate through the three-dimensional risk preference space. By comparing these results to other popular optimization frameworks, we will showcase a much more nuanced mapping of client preferences to portfolios. The chapter ends with a review of the sensitivity of our optimal portfolios to estimation error, highlighting generally robust asset allocation results.

There are three key assumptions made throughout this book to simplify the problem at hand dramatically without compromising the use case of the solution too severely: (1) we are only interested in managing portfolios over long-term horizons (10+ years); (2) consumption (i.e. withdrawals) out of investment portfolios only occurs after retirement; and (3) all assets deployed are extremely liquid. Let's quickly review the ramifications of these assumptions so the reader has a very clear perspective on the solution being built here.

Assumption 1 implies that we will not be focused on exploiting short-term (6–12 month) return predictability (AKA tactical asset allocation) or medium-term (3–5 year) return predictability (AKA opportunistic trading). Given the lack of tactical portfolio shifts, it is expected that advisors will typically hold positions beyond the short-term capital gains cutoff, and it can be assumed that taxes are not dependent on holding period, allowing us to account completely for taxes within our capital market forecasts. One can then assume there is little friction (tax or cost) to rebalancing at will, which leads to the following critical corollary: the long-term, multi-period portfolio decision can be reduced to the much simpler single period problem. Finally, the long horizon focus will help justify the deployment of historical distribution estimates as forecast starting points.

The first key ramification of assumption 2 is that we only need to consider "asset only" portfolio construction methods, i.e. asset-liability optimization methods with regular consumption within horizon (common for pension plans and insurance companies) are not considered. Additionally, it allows us to focus on the simpler problem of maximizing utility of wealth, rather than the more complex problem of maximizing utility of consumption.

Assumption 3 has two main consequences: (1) liquidity preferences can be ignored while setting the client risk profile; and (2) the liquidity risk premium need not be considered as a source of return. This assumption also keeps us squarely focused on the average retail client, since they don't have access to less-liquid alternative assets (like hedge funds and private equity/real estate) that are commonly held by ultra-high-net-worth individuals.

I hope this book and the accompanying software empowers advisors to tackle real-world asset allocation confidently on their own, with a powerful yet intuitive workflow.

David Berns
New York
January 10, 2020

Acknowledgments

First and foremost, thank you to my amazing family and friends for all their love and support throughout the writing of this book. Carolee, thank you for selflessly taking care of me and our family through all of the anxiety-laden early mornings, late nights, and weekend sessions; I couldn't have done this without you. Craig Enders, thank you for keeping me sane through this endeavor and being so helpful on just about every topic covered. Thank you to my trusted friends in the advisory space—Alex Chown, Jeff Egizi, Zung Nguyen, and Erick Rawlings—for all your thoughtful input. Thank you to Chad Buckendahl, Susan Davis-Becker, John Grable, Michael Guillemette, Michael Kitces, Mark Kritzman, Thierry Roncalli, and Jarrod Wilcox for helpful feedback on special topics. And thank you to Bill Falloon and the rest of the Wiley team for their gracious support and encouragement all along the way. I'd additionally like to thank Mark Kritzman, who through his lifelong commitment to rigorous yet elegant approaches in asset allocation, has inspired me to continue to advance a modern yet practical solution for our wealth management community. And finally, to my science teachers, Peggy Cebe, Leon Gunther, Will Oliver, and Terry Orlando, thank you for the lessons in research that I carry with me every day.

Modern Asset Allocation for Wealth Management

Preliminaries

The chapter begins with a review of two topics that will serve as the foundations of our asset allocation framework: *expected utility* and *estimation error*. Asset allocation is then defined as the process of maximizing expected utility while minimizing estimation error and its consequences—a simple yet powerful definition that will guide us through the rest of the book. The chapter concludes with an explicit definition of the modern yet tractable asset allocation framework that is recommended in this book: the maximization of a utility function with *not one but three* dimensions of client risk preferences while minimizing estimation error and its consequences by only investing in *distinct assets* and using *statistically sound historical estimates* as our forecasting foundation.

Key Takeaways:

1. Individual investors look to maximize their future utility of wealth, not their future wealth.
2. Mean-variance optimization is just an approximation to the full utility maximization problem we will tackle.
3. Maximizing the full utility function allows for a transparent and precise mapping of client preferences to portfolios.
4. A utility function with three risk preferences, accounting for both neoclassical and behavioral risk preferences, will be maximized in a returns-based framework.
5. Estimation error and the associated sensitivity to asset allocation recommendations can't be avoided or removed via a holy grail solution.
6. Estimation error will be managed by deploying non-parametric historical estimation of stationary assets with large sample sizes; and sensitivity to estimation error will be managed by only investing in easily distinguishable assets.

EXPECTED UTILITY

Introduction

When deciding whether to invest in an asset, at first glance one might think that the decision is as simple as calculating the expected value of the possible payoffs and investing if the expected payoff is positive. Let's say you are offered the opportunity to invest in a piece of property and the possible outcomes a year from now are a drop of $100,000 and a rise of $150,000, both with a 50% chance of occurring. The expected payoff for the investment is $25,000 (50% * −$100,000 + 50% * $150,000), so if you only care about expected return, then you would certainly invest.

But are you really prepared to potentially lose $100,000? The answer for many people is no, because $100,000 is a substantial fraction of their assets. If $100,000 represented all of your wealth, you certainly wouldn't risk losing everything. What about an extremely wealthy person? Should they necessarily be enthusiastic about this gamble since the potential loss represents only a small fraction of their wealth? Not if they are very averse to gambling and would much prefer just sitting tight with what they have ("a bird in the hand is worth two in the bush"). When making decisions regarding risky investments one needs to account for (1) how large the potential payoffs are relative to starting wealth; and (2) preferences regarding gambling.

In 1738 Daniel Bernoulli, one of the world's most gifted physicists and mathematicians at the time, posited that rational investors do not choose investments based on expected returns, but rather based on expected utility.[1] Utility is exactly what it sounds like: it is a personalized value scale one ascribes to a certain amount of wealth. For example, a very affluent person will not place the same value on an incremental $100 as someone less fortunate. And a professional gambler will not be as afraid of losing some of his wealth as someone who is staunchly opposed to gambling. The concept of utility can therefore account for both effects described in the previous paragraph: potential loss versus total wealth and propensity for gambling. The expected utility (EU) one period later in time is formally defined as

Equation 1.1 Expected Utility

$$EU = \sum_{i=1}^{O} p^i U^i$$

---

[1]Daniel Bernoulli was solving the now-famous St. Petersburg paradox posed by his cousin Nicolas in 1713: A casino offers a game where the player bets $1 and either loses it all or earns $2. If the player wins, the game is over, if the player loses, the game continues with double the bet size. The expected payoff is $1/2 * \$2 + 1/4 * \$4 + 1/8 * \$8 + \ldots = \infty$. What is a fair price of entry for such a game?

where p^i is the probability of outcome i, U^i is the utility of outcome i, and O is the number of possible outcomes.

Let's now return to our real estate example. Figure 1.1 shows an example utility function for a person with total wealth of $1 million. For the moment, don't worry about the precise shape of the utility function being used; just note that it is a reasonable one for many investors, as will be discussed later in the chapter. Initially the investor's utility is 1 (the utility units are arbitrary and are just an accounting tool[2]). Given the precise utility function being used and the starting wealth level relative to the potential wealth outcomes, the utility for the positive payoff outcome is 1.5 while the loss outcome has a utility of 0.29, and the expected utility of the investment is 0.9. Since the EU is less than the starting utility of 1, the bet should not be accepted, disagreeing with the decision to invest earlier based purely on expected payoff. If the utility function were a lot less curved downward (imagine more of a straight line at 45 degrees), indicative of an investor with greater propensity to gamble, the expected utility would actually be greater than 1 and the investor

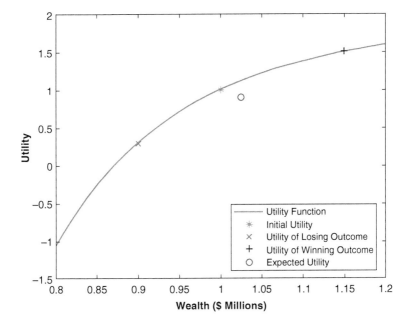

FIGURE 1.1　Choice Under Uncertainty: Expected Return vs. Expected Utility

---

[2]Utility functions are ordinal, which means that the actual value has no meaning, only the differences are useful. The fact that utility is purely a ranking tool is why utility functions are invariant to affine transformations (multiplying by a constant or adding a constant), a useful property we deploy later in the book.

would choose to make the investment. Additionally, if the starting wealth of the investor were much less than $1 million, the bet would become less appealing again, as the assumed utility function drops increasingly fast as wealth shrinks, bringing the expected utility well below the starting utility level. Hence, this simple utility construction can indeed account for both gambling propensity as well as the magnitude of the gamble relative to current wealth, as promised.

The concept of EU is easily extended to a portfolio of assets:

Equation 1.2 Portfolio Expected Utility

$$EU_{portfolio} = \sum_{i=1}^{O} p^i \sum_{j=1}^{N} w_j U_j^i = \sum_{i=1}^{O} p^i U_{port}^i$$

where we now first sum over all N assets in the portfolio according to their weights w_j, before summing over all O possible outcomes, which ultimately leads to the same formula as Eq. (1.1) except that each outcome is defined at the portfolio level U_{port}^i.

How can this help us choose an asset mix for clients? Since utility of wealth is what is important to clients, the goal of wealth management is to maximize the expected utility one period from now.[3,4] This is done by starting with Eq. (1.2) and filling in the blanks in four sequential steps: (1) specify the client's utility function; (2) choose assets to include in the portfolio; (3) delineate all possible outcomes and their probability over the next time period; and (4) find the portfolio weights that maximize future EU. These four steps are precisely what is covered in Chapters 2 through 5.

Before moving on, let's take stock of how incredibly insightful this succinct formulation is. The right side of Eq. (1.2) tells us that the advisor's entire mission when building a client's portfolio is to invest in a set of assets that have high probabilities of utility outcomes higher than starting utility (the higher the better) while having as low a probability as possible of outcomes below starting utility (again, the higher utility the better). Just how aggressive

---

[3]By maximizing utility one time step from now, as opposed to maximizing the change in utility from now to the next time step, we are making a subtle assumption that future utility of wealth can always be above the utility of current wealth. In other words, we assume there is a risk-free asset available to invest in that can always improve upon current utility.

[4]As discussed in the preface to this book, only the single period problem is considered, given our presumed ability to re-balance at will with little friction. Additionally, we focus on maximizing utility of wealth rather than consumption, assuming a lack of consumption pre-retirement.

we must be in accessing outcomes on the right side of the utility curve and avoiding those on the left is set by the shape of the utility function. For example, utility functions that fall off quickly to the left will require more focus on avoiding the negative outcomes while flatter functions will require less focus on negative outcome avoidance. If we can create an intuitive perspective on the shape of our client's utility function and the return distributions of the assets we invest in, we can build great intuition on the kinds of portfolios the client should have without even running an optimizer. This simple intuition will be a powerful guiding concept as we transition from modern portfolio theory (MPT), which is generally presented without mention of a utility function, to a completely general EU formulation of the problem.

MPT Is an Approximation

A key proposition of this book is to build client portfolios that have maximal EU as defined by Eq. (1.2). Conceptually, this is a very different approach than the popular mean-variance (M-V) framework, where portfolios are built by maximizing return while minimizing variance, without ever mentioning the client's utility. It is thus imperative to show how deploying the full utility function in the process of building portfolios relates to the MPT framework. It is also time to introduce the most complicated mathematical formula in the book. I promise that the temporary pain will be worth it in the long run and that the reader will not be subjected to any other formulas this complex for the remainder of the book.

The expected utility in our simple real estate example was a function of next period wealth. We will now transition to writing our next period utility outcomes U^i in Eq. (1.2) in terms of return r rather than wealth, by writing the next period wealth associated with an outcome i as $1 + r_i$. Our utility function is now a function of return instead of wealth. The utility function at a particular value of r can then be calculated as a function of successively higher order deviations (linear, squared, cubed, etc.) of r from its mean μ. Here is the formula for writing the utility as a function of the kth order deviation of return from the mean $(r - \mu)^k$:

Equation 1.3 Higher Order Expansion of Utility

$$U(r) = \sum_{k=0}^{\infty} \frac{1}{k!} U^{(k)}(r - \mu)^k$$

where $U^{(k)}$ is the kth order derivative of utility evaluated at $r = \mu$ and $k! = k * (k - 1) * (k - 2) * \ldots 2 * 1$, where $0! = 1$. For those familiar with calculus, this is just the Taylor series approximation of our utility function around the point μ, where the kth order derivative tells us how sensitive a function is to changes in the corresponding k^{th} order change in the underlying variable.

Let's take a look at the first couple of terms. The first term is the zeroth order approximation, where the zeroth order derivative is just the constant U(μ) and the zeroth order deviation is just 1, which is just our function value at r = μ, a great approximation to U(r) if r is close to μ. The second term then contains the first order approximation, which says that as r deviates from μ, the function roughly changes by the amount of the first derivative multiplied by linear changes in return relative to the mean (r − μ). Each successive term just brings in higher order derivatives and deviations to make additional adjustments to the series approximation of the full function.

The benefit of writing a function in terms of higher order deviations is that at some point the higher order terms become very small relative to the first few terms and can be ignored, which can often help simplify the problem at hand. This approximation should look familiar to anyone who has studied the sensitivity of bond prices to interest rates. A bond's price as a function of interest rates can be approximated via Eq. (1.3) by substituting bond price for utility and setting μ = 0. Then the first order bond price equals the current price (zeroth order term) plus the first derivative of bond price with respect to rates (bond duration) multiplied by the change in rates. For larger moves in interest rates one must then account for second order effects, which is just the second derivative of bond price with respect to rates (bond convexity) multiplied by squared changes in interest rates.

It is now time for the punchline of this section. Inserting Eq. (1.3) into Eq. (1.2), the expected utility for a portfolio of assets can be written as:

Equation 1.4 Utility as a Function of Moments

$$EU_{portfolio} = U^{(1)}\mu_{port} + \frac{1}{2}U^{(2)}\sigma_{port}^2 + \frac{1}{6}U^{(3)}s_{port}^3 + \frac{1}{24}U^{(4)}\kappa_{port}^4 + \ldots$$

an infinite series we are only showing the first four[5] terms of. $U^{(k)}$ is the kth order derivative of utility evaluated at r = μ_{port}, μ_{port} is the portfolio expected return, σ_{port} is the portfolio expected volatility, s_{port} is the portfolio expected

---

[5]Here, and for the remainder of the book, whenever we have cause to study the individual moments of a distribution, we will only consider the first four moments because estimation of fifth and higher moments is extremely challenging (a reality that will become evident in Chapter 4 when we review estimation error of moments) and, more importantly, the effects of these terms will be negligibly small.

skew, and κ_{port} is the portfolio expected kurtosis. In statistics, these last four quantities are also known as the first, second, third, and fourth "moments" of the portfolio's distribution of returns, since the kth moment is defined as the expected value of $(r - \mu)^k$.

Any return distribution can be completely characterized by its full set of moments, as each moment provides incrementally distinct information about the shape of the return distribution, almost as if each moment is like a partial fingerprint of the distribution. The first moment describes the location of the center of the distribution; the second moment describes the width of the distribution; the third and fourth moments characterize how asymmetric and fat-tailed the distribution is, respectively. It is expected that the reader is familiar with the first two moments but not the next two, which are reviewed in depth in the following section.

Upon solving for the expected value of the series approximation to a utility function, the kth order deviation turned into the kth order moment, an exciting turn of events. Equation (1.4) demonstrates that the maximization of portfolio EU, the core goal for any wealth manager, amounts to maximizing over an infinite set of moments. A typical utility function we will consider will have a positive first derivative and negative second derivative (much more on this later). Therefore, when typically maximizing EU, we are searching for maximal portfolio return and minimal portfolio variance while also maximizing an infinite set of other portfolio return moments whose derivatives (and resulting signs in Eq. (1.4)) are to be determined. MPT is now clearly an approximation to the full EU maximization process we really want to consider! The M-V optimization solution is what is known as a "second order" approximation to the full solution, since it only considers the first two terms of the problem.

In the following section we review the conditions under which we should be concerned with higher order terms missing in M-V, and from there we show precisely how we are going to approach the problem without making a second order approximation (completely avoiding what is formally known as "approximation error") (Adler & Kritzman, 2007; Grinold, 1999). We are in good company here: Markowitz himself has said that if mean-variance is not applicable, then the appropriate solution is the maximization of the full utility function (Markowitz, 2010).

For all readers who have made it to this point, thank you for bearing with me through the most mathematical part of the book. At this point you no longer have to worry about Eq. (1.3), which was solely introduced to derive Eq. (1.4), the key result of the section and one that will be used throughout the book. I encourage any readers not fully comfortable with Eq. (1.4) to go back and reread this section, noting that Eq. (1.3) is a mathematical complexity that can be glossed over as long as Eq. (1.4) is fully baked into your psyche.

Higher Moment Motivation

It was just shown that MPT is a second order approximation to the full problem we ideally want to solve. A natural question now is whether the chopped off third and higher terms that MPT is missing is a critical deficiency. If it is, then the maximization of the full utility function becomes a necessity. But it is quite hard to generalize the answer to the question, since it is highly dependent on the utility function of the client, and the expected moments of the assets being deployed; and we will not have those answers for a few more chapters still. Even then the answers will vary for every single client and portfolio, and will even change over time as capital markets evolve.

At this stage, though, we are focused on motivating a compelling asset allocation framework; hence the key question we must address is whether there is a chance for higher order terms to come into play. To this end, it should be noted that higher order terms do not exist in Eq. (1.4) unless two criteria are met: (1) portfolio return distributions have third or higher moments; and (2) our utility function has a preference regarding those higher moments (i.e. it has non-zero third order derivatives or higher). By studying higher moment properties of some typical investable assets and higher order preferences embedded in typical utility functions, you will see that both conditions are generally met, and higher order terms should be accounted for in the process.

Before we tackle the first condition by investigating whether typical assets have higher moment characteristics, let's first build up our general understanding of the third and fourth moments—skew and kurtosis, respectively. The easiest way to think about higher moments is to start from the most common distribution in mother nature, the normal distribution.[6] The important thing to know about the normal distribution is that it is symmetric about the mean (skew = 0), and its tails are not too skinny and are not too fat (kurtosis = 3). Figure 1.2 shows a normal distribution of monthly returns, with mean of 1% and volatility of 2%; this will serve as our baseline distribution, to which we will now add higher moments.

The easiest way to intuit the effect of negative skew is to imagine a tall tree, firmly rooted in the ground and standing up perfectly straight. If one were to try to pull the tree out of the ground by tying a rope to the top of the tree and pulling to the right, the top of the tree would begin to move right and the roots on the left side of the tree would start to come out of the ground while the roots on the right side would get compressed deeper into

---

[6]Fun fact: the normal distribution is so common in our universe due to the Central Limit Theorem, a mathematical proof that shows that a large sum of random variables, no matter how they are individually distributed, will be normally distributed.

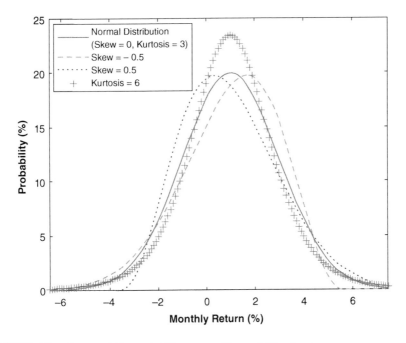

FIGURE 1.2 Skew and Kurtosis Effects on a Normal Distribution

the ground. This is why in Figure 1.2 the peak of the distribution with skew of −0.5 is slightly right of the normal distribution peak while the left tail is now raised a bit and the right tail is cut off slightly. Hence, a negatively skewed distribution has a higher frequency of extremely bad events than a normal distribution while the number of events just above the mean goes up and the number of extreme positive events goes down. Positive skew is the exact opposite of the situation just described (a tree now being pulled out to the left): positive skew distributions have a higher frequency of extremely favorable events than a normal distribution while the number of events just below the mean goes up and the number of extreme negative events goes down.

Kurtosis, on the other hand, is a symmetrical effect. The way I intuit kurtosis above 3 is to imagine wrapping my hand around the base of a normal distribution and squeezing, which forces some of the middle of the distribution out into the tails (through the bottom of my fist) and some of the middle of the distribution up (through the top of my fist). Therefore, a kurtosis above 3 implies, relative to a normal distribution, more events in both tails, more events at the very center of the distribution, and less middle-of-the-road events. Decreasing kurtosis from 3 then has the exact opposite effect: fewer events will happen in the tails and in the very center of the distribution relative to a normal distribution, in exchange for more mediocre positive and negative outcomes. Figure 1.2 shows a distribution with a kurtosis of 6, where you clearly see an increase in the number of events in the middle of the distribution at the expense of fewer middle-of-the-road deviations from the mean; and with a bit more strain you can see the increased number of tail events (the signature "fat tails" of high kurtosis distributions). This moment may remind you of the second moment (volatility), due to its symmetry. But note that volatility controls the width of the distribution everywhere while kurtosis has different effects on the width of the distribution at the top, middle, and bottom: when we raised kurtosis from 3 to 6, the width of the distribution widened at the top, shrank in the middle, and widened at the very bottom.

Now that we are familiar with skew and kurtosis, let's return to the first point we would like to prove. To simplify things, we will not be looking at portfolio higher moments; instead, we will look at the higher moments of the underlying assets. While this is not the precise condition we are out to prove, the existence of asset-level higher moments should certainly put us on alert for the existence of portfolio-level higher moments.[7]

Figure 1.3 plots the third and fourth moments for some common publicly traded assets, where we clearly see that most assets indeed have higher moments associated with their distributions; therefore QED on our first point.[8,9] But let's pause and make sure we understand the results. For instance, why do 3 Month Treasuries have such extreme positive skew? And why do equities show up on the opposite side of the skew spectrum?

Given our understanding of how positively skewed distributions are shaped, it is hopefully rather intuitive why short-term US Treasuries are positively skewed: they have very limited left tail risk given their minimal

---

[7]One may be tempted to assume that the existence of asset-level higher moments is a necessary condition for portfolio-level higher moments. While it is true that one can't have portfolio-level variance without asset-level variance, the same is not true for higher moments, an effect that will be on full display in Chapter 3.

[8]Another fun piece of evidence we have on this front is that the CAPM (Sharpe, 1964), a purely second order model that relates return to volatility, was improved upon by introducing skew (Kraus & Litzenberger, 1976), validating the existence of the third moment. We will shortly use this same model as evidence that investors indeed have clearly defined preferences regarding skew.

[9]For those familiar with the Jarque-Bera test for non-normality, every asset presented in Figure 1.3 failed the test at the 0.1% significance level, implying that there is less than a 0.1% chance that we are flagging these assets as non-normal while they are actually normal.

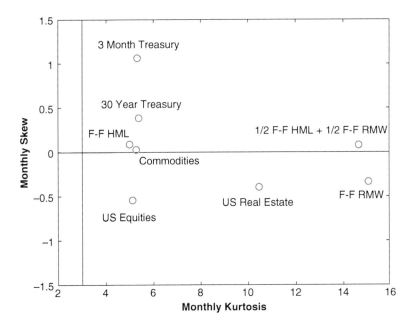

FIGURE 1.3 Skew and Kurtosis of Common Modern Assets (Historical Data from 1972 to 2018)[10]

duration or credit risk while simultaneously offering the potential for some outsized moves to the upside as a flight-to-quality play during times of stress. At the other extreme is US equities, an asset class that intuitively leaves the investor susceptible to negative skew via extreme liquidity events like the Great Recession. Figure 1.3 also shows a of couple long/short alternative risk premia assets: the Fama-French value factor (F-F HML) and the Fama-French robustness factor (F-F RMW), along with a strategy that is split 50/50 between these two factors. As you can see, these market-neutral equity strategies have the ability to introduce both positive skew and kurtosis relative to their underlying equity universe.

In Chapter 3 we will spend time reviewing the landscape of risk premia, and in that process we will build a generalized understanding of how skew is introduced to investment strategies. As you will see then, I believe that

---

[10]Treasuries are represented by constant maturity indices from the Center for Research in Security Prices at the University of Chicago's Booth School of Business (CRSP®); equity data is from Ken French's online library, with all factor assets following conventional definitions; real estate is represented by the FTSE Nareit US Real Estate Index; and commodities are expressed via the S&P GSCI Commodity Index.

one of the key innovations within investment products over the next few decades will be increasingly surgical vehicles for accessing higher moments (via alternative risk premia), a key motivation for the inclusion of higher moments in our asset allocation framework.

Let's now move to the second minimum condition to care about higher moments: clients must have preferences when it comes to higher moments; that is, a client's utility function must be sensitive to the third moment or higher. For now we will analyze this question generally, as we have still not formally introduced the utility function we will be deploying.

Empirical work on the higher moment capital asset pricing model (CAPM) (Kraus & Litzenberger, 1976) was one of the first lines of research that showed us that investors prefer positive skew by virtue of requiring compensation for negative skew. Just as the CAPM showed us that expected returns increase with volatility (investors demand higher returns to hold more volatile assets), the higher moment extension of CAPM shows us that expected returns increase as skew becomes increasingly negative (investors demand higher returns to hold more negatively skewed assets).

It has also been shown that if our utility function is such that the investor always prefers more wealth to less (utility is always increasing with wealth/return), and that the benefit of extra wealth fades as wealth increases (the slope of your utility function gets less and less positive with wealth/return), we have preferences for positive skew and negative excess kurtosis (Scott & Horvath, 1980).[11] And the result is even more powerful than that: these assumptions allow you to draw the conclusion that an investor should prefer all odd moments to be high and all even moments to be low! We have arrived at a key result very rigorously, and at the same time the even versus odd preference seems to be rather intuitive for a rational investor. As reviewed earlier in the chapter, a rational investor wants to earn money while avoiding the risk of ruin and without gambling beyond their preferred limits, which is just saying that a rational investor prefers high returns while avoiding drawdowns and dispersion. Hence, an optimal portfolio for a rational investor would have large returns (large first moment), minimal drawdowns (large third moment and small fourth moment), and minimal dispersion (low second moment), showcasing a clear preference for odd moments and an aversion to even moments. But let's pause our discussion on higher moment preferences until we have introduced the precise utility function we will deploy. Hopefully we have

---

[11] Excess kurtosis is just kurtosis minus 3, a handy nomenclature given that we often want to reference kurtosis relative to the normal distribution. Negative excessive kurtosis implies kurtosis less than 3 and positive excessive kurtosis implies kurtosis greater than 3.

motivated the fact that under a simple set of assumptions about client utility (which you will see shortly often applies to real-world utility functions), individuals will have clear preferences toward higher moments and we don't want to ignore these preferences.

At this point we have shown that many common assets have statistically significant higher moments, and that clients will often have well-defined preferences to higher moments, validating that we should indeed be wary that higher moments could play a role in building client portfolios. But we have not yet discussed the magnitudes of the higher order utility derivatives or portfolio moments, which determine the size of the higher order terms relative to the first two terms in Eq. (1.4), and ultimately inform whether these terms play a meaningful role in the EU maximization problem. As seen first-hand in the portfolios we create in Chapter 5, today's most common asset classes and their particular expected returns often lead to an EU solution that is predominantly a simple tradeoff between return and volatility. Hence, despite the fact that utility functions generally have higher moment preferences and assets are typically non-normal, the higher order terms can often have minimal effects. Unfortunately, it is impossible to know this, a priori, for a given client utility and investment universe. The only way to know for sure is to deploy the full utility function and analyze the results, which is clearly a reasonable prerequisite given the preceding presentation. The expected moments will also change in time as market environments ebb and flow. If, all of a sudden, return forecasts are cut across the board while the utility function and assets deployed are unchanged, higher order terms that were once inconsequential could potentially become relevant—a complete unknown until we are actually there.

As you will see in Chapter 3, there appears to be a natural evolution in the asset management industry toward investment products that are more focused on the exploitation of higher moments, where we would expect an increase in the number of assets whose higher moments can indeed influence the asset allocation decision. We have already seen the first generation of this trend make its way to the retail space in the form of style premia and option strategies, both born in the land of hedge funds, where higher moments are a key input to any asset allocation process (Cremers, Kritzman, & Page, 2004). And given the ease with which we can run optimizers over the full utility function these days, there is little computational hurdle to deploying a framework that avoids lower-order approximations.

Modernized Preference Motivation

The most pressing issue with MPT in today's markets and for a typical retail client is not the missing higher order terms in Eq. (1.4). Rather, it is the more practical question of how to find the second derivative of utility,[12] which plays a critical role in setting the precise portfolios that MPT recommends for clients. It turns out that once behavioral risk preferences are accounted for (introduced in the next section), a singular measure of risk preference is insufficient.

Let's assume that markets are fully described by the first two moments. The second derivative in Eq. (1.4) is a measure of a client's aversion to volatility (with a negative sign pulled out in front of it), which many practitioners intuit for their clients as they get to know them personally or through some form of risk tolerance questionnaire. Advisors then assign a client to one of four or five volatility-targeted portfolios on the M-V efficient frontier (clients with lower perceived risk aversion will be assigned a portfolio with higher volatility, and vice versa). I have no issue with the fact that clients are generally only binned into four or five buckets, since estimation error often prevents much more granular assignments, as reviewed in Chapter 5. Nor, at the moment, am I flagging the methods of measuring preferences just described (although I do believe the more mathematical system laid out in Chapter 2 for measuring risk preferences is superior to the standard qualitative questionnaire, and certainly better than an intuitive read of a client). I am also not flagging the sole use of a second order approximation, where clients are binned solely by their volatility, since for this exercise I am assuming markets are fully described by the first two moments. Rather, I have issue with the second derivative being assessed as a singular number.

In the following section we will introduce our modern utility function, which has three parameters, including the traditional (rational) risk aversion parameter, along with two behavioral (irrational) parameters. Then, in Chapter 2, we will show that to account for financial goals we must moderate the three preferences. A critical feature of our goals moderation system is that each parameter must be moderated independently; therefore we cannot simply lump them into a single volatility aversion. Indeed, if our client had no financial goals, we could just measure the full utility function and fit it for a constant second derivative, avoiding the specification of a utility function that requires careful delineation between three different preference types. The inclusion of financial goals in the presence of irrational risk preferences

---

[12]In MPT the aversion to volatility is a constant known as "risk aversion," but in our more general utility function framework this traditional parameter is just one of three parameters that can affect the second derivative of utility. Hence, we reserve the term "risk aversion" to refer to the constant coefficient specifically in MPT, and not the second derivative of utility in general. In Chapter 5 the utility second derivative will be referred to as "generalized risk aversion," as it captures volatility preferences beyond the traditional risk aversion parameter.

requires us to fully divorce ourselves from MPT. If this is confusing right now, don't despair; Chapters 2 and 5 will make it clearer.

With that said, even in the absence of financial goals, I believe it is wise still to deploy the fully utility function introduced in the following section. Its three distinct risk preference parameters provide a rich amount of detail that an advisor can work through with his or her client. In addition to providing a very accurate assessment of the client's utility function and all its derivatives, this modern tool also allows both advisor and client to understand quickly the client's risk preferences in a powerful and intuitive framework. So, even in the case of no financial goals, one can gain a lot of intuition around the subtle behaviors that create utility curvature by measuring our three risk preferences and painting a full picture behind the singular volatility aversion parameter.

Of course, in the cases where higher moments indeed matter, the full utility function will indeed provide additional higher moment preference information that is relevant.

As you will see starting in Chapter 2 (and starkly punctuated in our discussions in Chapter 5), by combining modern perspectives on utility functions with the full utility optimization routine, we will generate a very nuanced but intuitive and accurate prescription for matching client preferences and goals to an appropriate portfolio.

A Modern Utility Function

It is now time to introduce the utility function we will deploy for the remainder of the book. Utility functions are completely unfamiliar to us in our everyday life, so it is imperative that we connect this mathematical representation of risk preferences to clearly identifiable and intuitive behaviors. To this end, I begin with a review of the simplest utility function that may satisfy a client's preferences, and then iteratively introduce two modifications to that function to account for two additional types of risk preferences. The section concludes with the formal definition of a generalized utility function, which we will use for the remainder of the book to succinctly capture all three "dimensions" of risk preferences that are key for building portfolios.[13]

---

[13] In reality, a client's utility function is as unique and complex as their fingerprint, and could certainly be specified with more nuance by deploying more than three parameters or not even using parameters but specifying the entire utility function piece by piece. I purposely choose to deploy the specific utility presented in this section, with its three defining parameters, given the clear connection each parameter has to an intuitive client behavior (hence promoting clear intuition behind the utility function), and the rich amount of academic literature on these three parameters that will help guide us through their usage.

The traditional (AKA neoclassical) utility function used in economics for rational investors is the power utility, with its single parameter risk aversion γ:

Equation 1.5 Power Utility

$$U = 2 - W^{(1-\gamma)}$$

where W is the single period wealth change $1 + r$, r is the single period portfolio return (we drop the "port" subscript from here on since for the remainder of the book we will only be considering utility outcomes for a portfolio of assets), and γ is parameterized between 1.5 and 12 (as detailed in Chapter 2).[14] Power utility is plotted as a function of r in Figure 1.4 with $\gamma = 6$ and is precisely the same utility function plotted in Figure 1.1.

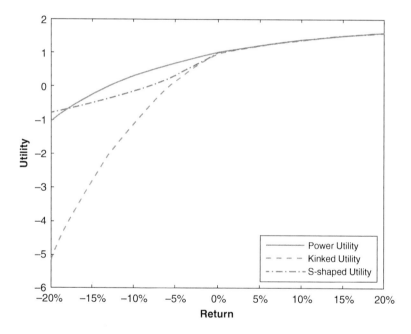

FIGURE 1.4 Graphical Representation of Utility Functions ($\gamma = 6, \lambda = 3$)

---

[14]Two notes on this function for those interested: (1) The standard form of this function is W^c/c, where c is a constant, which we have rewritten in terms of the (constant relative) risk aversion $\gamma = 1 - c$; (2) We have deployed an affine transformation to remove the scaling by γ so that some of the tools we deploy in Chapter 3 are easily comparable across risk aversions (see discussion on contribution to utility).

This function fulfills the two key intuitive attributes we require from our baseline utility function, which happen to be the exact same attributes required earlier to be able to say a client always prefers high odd moments and low even moments:

1. More wealth is always preferred (utility first derivative is always positive).
2. The benefit of extra wealth fades as wealth increases; that is, at low wealth levels, losing a little hurts a lot (utility second derivative is always negative).

It is interesting to note that this function, which was the darling of economists for most of the twentieth century, is well approximated by Markowitz's simple mean-variance framework for low levels of risk aversion or highly normal return distributions (Cremers, Kritzman, & Page, 2004). This key fact, combined with the solvability of M-V on the earliest of modern computers, explains why mean-variance has been so dominant in the world of asset allocation. But this function, by virtue of being well represented by the MPT solution, roughly has no opinion on skew or higher moments. It is probably safe to assume that no rational investor, even if their risk aversion is on the low end of the spectrum, is agnostic to even moderate levels of negative skew; so it is hard to accept power utility as our core utility function. As an example, look at both principal and agent responses to the Great Recession: many clients and advisors need portfolios that avoid large exposure to negative skew to be able to keep them invested in a long-term plan.

A kinked utility function, with its two parameters, risk aversion γ and loss aversion λ (parameterized here from 1.5 to 12 and 1 to 3, as detailed in Chapter 2), satisfies our two simple criteria while additionally having the practical third moment sensitivity we require:[15]

Equation 1.6 Kinked Utility

$$U = \begin{cases} 2 - W^{(1-\gamma)} \ for \ r \geq 0 \\ 2 - \lambda \ W^{(1-\gamma)} \ for \ r < 0 \end{cases}$$

As you can see, kinked utility is the same as the power utility when returns are positive; but when returns are negative, the utility drops at a rate

---

[15] For presentation purposes we drop a constant term from this formula that is embedded in all calculations presented and accounts for the discontinuous nature of the function: $-1^{(1-\gamma)} + \lambda^{(1-\gamma)}$.

λ times as fast, giving us clear preference toward positive skew (and away from negative skew) when λ is greater than 1 (when λ equals 1 this function is the same as Eq. (1.5)). Figure 1.4 shows the kinked utility with risk aversion $\gamma = 6$ and loss aversion $\lambda = 3$, where you can clearly see the kinked utility drop faster than the power utility with the same risk aversion in the loss domain, since $\lambda = 3$. But admittedly, at this point we are just postulating this specific form for an asymmetric utility function. Can we justify the kinked utility function with more than just our intuition on investor preferences to negative skew?

Enter prospect theory (PT) (Kahneman & Taversky, 1979), a key advance in our understanding of real-world risk preferences from the discipline of behavioral economics, where psychology meets economics. This descriptive theory of real human behavior introduces two new "irrational" features of decision-making under uncertainty to the "rational" theory encapsulated by our power utility function.

The first is "loss aversion," where an investor feels the emotional drain of losses disproportionately more than they feel the emotional benefit of gains. The more loss aversion one has, the more unwilling they will be to play a game with very favorable terms if there is the possibility of losing even a small amount of money. For example, someone with strong loss aversion would not flip a coin where they stood to win $100 on heads and lose $20 on tails, a very favorable game that any robot (AKA neoclassical investor) would happily play.

The second PT feature is "reflection," where investors are risk averse only when it comes to gains and are risk seeking when it comes to losses. Unlike the power utility function investor, who always prefers their current situation to a 50/50 chance of winning or losing the same amount (since the utility second derivative is negative), an investor with reflection will actually favor the aforementioned 50/50 gamble if they are in a losing situation. For example, a client with reflection who owns a stock with a paper loss of 20%, where from here the stock can either get back to even or drop another 20%, would choose to roll the dice, whereas a client who is risk averse across both loss and gain domains would not risk the possibility of further loss. Another way to think of reflection is that it represents the joint emotions of "hoping to avoid losses" (risk-seeking in the loss domain) while being "afraid of missing out on gains" (risk-averse in the gain domain), which precisely agrees with the well-known phenomenon where amateur traders cut winners too quickly and hold onto losers too long.

Both PT effects require us to shift from thinking of utility in terms of wealth to thinking in terms of gains and losses, since both new preference features require a clear distinction between losses and gains.[16] For a gentle yet detailed overview of PT, see Levy's review (Levy, 1992).[17] But for a quick and intuitive overview, a fantastic description of PT was provided to me by my father, who, upon completing the risk preference diagnostics I review in Chapter 2, turned to me and said, "I don't like risk, but I like to win." This statement validates the risk profile I have developed for my father over 40 years of getting to know him. It also perfectly represents the average PT client, who "doesn't like risk" (which I interpret as including both risk and loss aversion) but "likes to win" (which I interpret as being risk-seeking in the loss domain in an effort to avoid realizing a loss). And yes, my father's risk preference questionnaire results clearly flagged him for both loss aversion and reflection.

The kinked utility function already introduced indeed addresses prospect theory's loss aversion effect precisely; therefore we have grounded that iteration of our utility function on solid behavioral research grounds. But what about reflection? The S-shaped utility function will do the trick. To continue down our intuitive path connecting power to kinked to S-shaped utility as we introduce new dimensions of risk preferences, I again stitch together two power functions across the gain and loss domains, with some simplified parameterization to construct the S-shaped utility:[18]

Equation 1.7 S-Shaped Utility

$$U = \begin{cases} 2 - W^{(1-\gamma)} \ for \ r \geq 0 \\ 2 + \lambda \left(2 - W\right)^{(1-\gamma)} \ for \ r < 0 \end{cases}$$

---

[16]PT actually allows loss aversion and reflection to take place around any "reflection point," not necessarily a return of zero. Here, we follow generally accepted practices and define our reference point as the "status quo" (zero return); hence, all PT effects we discuss reference gains versus losses.

[17]PT also states that people overweight the likelihood of very unlikely events, a phenomenon captured in PT by "decision weights," which moderate the objective probability weights used in calculating the utility function. I ignore this effect because I view probability assignment as a behavior that is naturally moderated (see Chapter 2) by virtue of advisors being the ones setting capital markets assumptions (which includes both outcome delineation and probability assignments). PT also has an "editing" stage for any decision process, at which point the problem at hand is defined and choices are delineated, again assumed to be completely managed by the advisor within the framework of this book.

[18]As we did for kinked utility, for presentation purposes we drop a constant term from this formula that is embedded in all calculations presented and accounts for the discontinuous nature of the function: $-1^{(1-\gamma)} - \lambda^{(1-\gamma)}$.

This function has the same two parameters as the kinked function, risk aversion γ and loss aversion λ, but now in the domain of losses our utility function actually curves up rather than going down, resembling the shape of the letter "S." Figure 1.4 shows the S-shaped utility function with $\gamma = 6$ and $\lambda = 3$. One can clearly see the function fall off faster than the power function as you first enter the loss domain due to the loss aversion of 3; but as you proceed further into the loss domain the function curves up due to the reflection embodied in the S-shaped function, which implies a preference for risk on the downside. Note that we have assumed that the reflection effect is symmetric (i.e. we have the same γ in both gain and loss domains). You can indeed make this S-shaped function more complicated by assuming asymmetric curvature in the gain and loss domains, but in an effort to keep the story simple we will assume the same curvature parameter γ in both domains. While studies have shown that population averages of loss and gain domain curvature are very symmetric, there can indeed be significant departure from symmetry at the individual level (Kahneman & Taversky, 1979; Abdellaoui, Bleichrodt, & Paraschiv, 2007), a feature an advisor may wish to capture if it doesn't add too much burden to their measurement process and presentation to clients.

In order to systematically capture all three client risk preferences we have reviewed thus far via a single utility function, we define a generalized utility function that can fluidly evolve based on all three dimensions of risk preferences:[19]

Equation 1.8 Three-Dimensional Risk Profile Utility Function

$$U = \begin{cases} 2 - W^{(1-\gamma)} \ for\ r \geq 0 \\ 2 - \lambda\ W^{(1-\gamma)} \ for\ r < 0, \varphi = 0 \\ 2 + \lambda\ (2 - W)^{(1-\gamma)} \ for\ r < 0, \varphi = 1 \end{cases}$$

This function has both risk aversion γ and loss aversion λ, but now there is one additional parameter φ, which takes on the value of 1 when reflection should be expressed, and 0 when there is no reflection. Equation (1.8) is our final utility function, which collapses to Eq. (1.7) when $\varphi = 1$, collapses to Eq. (1.6) when $\varphi = 0$, and collapses to Eq. (1.5) when $\varphi = 0$ and $\lambda = 1$. From here on out we will solely reference our three-dimensional risk profile utility

---

[19]For presentation purposes we continue to drop a constant term from this formula that is embedded in all calculations presented: $-1^{(1-\gamma)} - \phi\lambda^{(1-\gamma)} + (1 - \phi)\lambda^{(1-\gamma)}$.

defined in Eq. (1.8), as it fully encapsulates all three dimensions (γ, λ, and φ) of a modern client risk profile.

Earlier in the chapter we argued generally that client preference would be for higher skew and lower kurtosis. The power and kinked utility functions indeed preserve that general preference for odd moments and aversion to even moments, since their first derivative is always positive (utility always increases with return) and their second derivative is always negative (utility is always concave). However, with the introduction of reflection we must reassess that set of preferences. For our three-dimensional risk profile utility when $\varphi = 1$, these preferences now depend on all three parameter choices (Cremers, Kritzman, & Page, 2004), as the second derivative is no longer negative for all returns, and preference moments will be determined by the competing forces of risk aversion, loss aversion, and reflection. The bottom line is that moment preferences depend on the precise parameters of our three-dimensional risk profile utility function, where we know those preferences only with certainty when $\varphi = 0$. With that said, we do not have to harp on the topic of moment preferences any longer, as the core proposition of this book is to maximize the expected utility, which automatically accounts for all higher moment preferences; hence advisors need not dissect individual moment preferences for their clients. Hopefully, though, the discussion of moment preferences has added some interesting color around the nuances of the utility function we will be deploying.

In Chapter 2, 1 will review how to set our utility function parameters γ, λ, and φ. But before we move away from our discussion on maximizing utility, let's discuss how we will actually go about maximizing the full utility function, and not just optimizing a lower order approximation.

Returns-Based EU Maximization

Clearly the real asset allocation problem we want to solve is the maximization of the full utility function. But what exactly does that look like when the rubber meets the road? In the classic MPT solution we input expected returns, variances, and covariances into an optimizer to find portfolios that maximize expected returns while minimizing expected variance, which can conveniently be plotted as a 2-D efficient frontier. But what are the inputs into the optimizer when maximizing EU? And what outputs are we plotting in the case of the full utility, if there are no moments to speak of?

Equation (1.2) is the precise definition of what we will now be maximizing: expected utility over all possible outcomes. But how exactly do you define an outcome in the maximization of EU across a set of assets? An outcome is simply one possible joint outcome of all assets (i.e. the returns for all assets during the same period). From here on we will use a monthly return period to define an outcome, since this is roughly the period over which client-concerning drawdowns can generally occur. Hence, we formally define a single outcome as the returns for all our assets during a single month. We can then calculate the portfolio utility U^i for each outcome i, defined by an exhaustive set of monthly joint return outcomes (AKA the joint return distribution) and our client's utility function, which is a function of the portfolio asset allocation (what we are solving for, AKA the decision variable). Once we set the probability p^i for each outcome, we can run an optimizer that will find the weights of the assets in the portfolio that maximize the expected value of utility over all outcomes.

But how do we create a complete list of possible outcomes and their probabilities? To facilitate generation of future outcomes we will utilize the entire set of historical outcomes. The returns for our assets during an individual month in history will represent a single outcome, where the full historical set of months will represent all possible outcomes, and we will assume equal-weighted probability for each outcome. Chapter 4 is fully dedicated to validating our use of historical joint returns as a starting point for our outcome forecasts, where we will also provide techniques for manipulating the outcomes to account for personalized market forecasts, taxes, and other key adjustments.

Returns-based optimization has been around for a long time, and while it may sound complex or esoteric, it is really neither. I personally think this concept is rather simple once it is grasped. It connects in a very natural way the investment portfolio to the actual thing we care about, our client's utility. Just think about how intuitive our real estate example was at the beginning of the chapter. There was no discussion of moments, just a couple of possible outcomes and a utility function that helped make our choice. I also think it's beautifully elegant in the way it collapses away all discussions of moments by calculating the U^i, which accounts for all possible asset and cross-asset information. It never ceases to amaze me that every subtle relationship between assets, whether linear (covariance) or non-linear (coskewness, cokurtosis, etc.), is captured by the sequential list of joint return outcomes.

Before we leave this high-level discussion of our optimization framework, I want to point out that you will not see any efficient frontiers in this book. As alluded to earlier when discussing client risk preference measurements, a key benefit of a mean-variance efficient frontier is that one can bin clients into different sections of the frontier based on volatility targets, which helps avoid a more formal/mathematical description of the client's aversion to volatility. But in our approach, we begin by precisely diagnosing the client's preferences as defined by our three utility parameters and then run the optimizer for the singular utility function defined by the client's personal parameters, producing just a single portfolio that is appropriate for our client. This approach completely avoids having to create all possible optimal portfolios and then slotting a client into one of them; hence the lack of need for an efficient frontier. This may sound pedantic, but the distinction is rather important regarding the accuracy of our process for defining client preferences. As you will see, in a framework characterized by well-defined and intuitive risk preference parameters, we will have more reason to plot all possible portfolios as a function of the three utility parameters than to plot them as a function of one or more moments.

ESTIMATION ERROR

Introduction

Anyone who has attempted to run a quantitative asset allocation process that deploys an optimizer is very aware of how sensitive the results can be to the assumptions. In the case of mean-variance optimization, it is well known that relatively small changes in return expectations can cause dramatic changes in the recommended asset allocation of the optimizer. Figure 1.5 shows the recommended asset allocation of a mean-variance optimizer for two assets, US large cap equities and US small cap equities, as a function of the expected

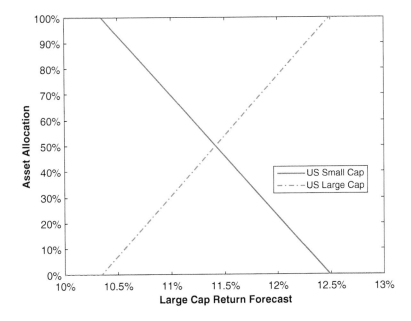

FIGURE 1.5 Allocation Sensitivity to Forecasts

annual return for US large caps that is fed into the optimizer.[20] As you can see, only a 2% shift in return expectation flips the recommended portfolio from all small cap to all large cap. This kind of sensitivity is an incredibly large hurdle for widespread adoption of optimized asset allocation frameworks, since it prevents users from gaining confidence that the optimization process is a worthwhile exercise.

Can we assign blame here? Is the optimizer an overly sensitive tool that needs to be treated with great care or do users of optimizers need to be world-class forecasters who can stand behind the resulting optimizer prescription regardless of its sensitivity? The answer is both. Ideally we would have forecasts that are 100% accurate, which have zero error bars around them (i.e. they have zero estimation error), and we can let the optimizer loose with full confidence. But this is never the case and we additionally want our optimizer to not be overly sensitive to the error bars on our inputs. Thus there are two topics that must be tackled by advisors: how to minimize estimation error and how to minimize the sensitivity to estimation error. Let's begin with estimation error itself and how to minimize it.

Minimizing Estimation Error

The ideal situation for anyone trying to forecast the long-term behavior of a random process, such as the joint monthly return stream for a universe of investable assets over long horizons (10+ years) as we are doing here, is to know that the distribution of the process we have seen in the past is precisely the distribution we will see in the future.[21] In this instance we know what statisticians call the "true" distribution, and everything we can know about the process is contained in its historical distribution. In this case one can just use the measured distribution as their forecast and they would have a perfect estimate (zero estimation error).

---

[20]Our US small and large cap assets are just the top and bottom quintile portfolios from Ken French's online library of market size portfolios. We then deployed historical mean and covariance estimates based on data from 1972–2018 and varied the forecast for large caps around the historical mean. We also assume a low level of risk aversion in this example.

[21]It is important to reiterate that if our forecasting horizon was very short (say a few months), we would not get very precise forecasts using the historical distribution, since individual months are highly idiosyncratic realizations of a large distribution of possible events. The main reason we can confidently deploy historical results here is our horizon is very long—one of three key assumptions laid out in the preface—and we are looking to estimate hundreds of months of outcomes where the distribution of events is indeed then what matters.

Using historical data for your forecast in this manner is known as non-parametric estimation, since one doesn't specify any functional forms or parameters during the estimation process, and you have completely avoided any approximation error (similar to what we are doing by using the full utility function instead of M-V). Given the lack of any function or parameter specification, this technique also qualifies as the simplest of all estimation techniques. Therefore, non-parametric estimation from a true distribution is simultaneously the most accurate and the simplest forecasting technique possible. The rub here is the assumption that we are looking at the true distribution. How do we know we have measured the true return distribution of the asset and not just a moderately representative sample of the true distribution?

We now introduce the two key concepts that help answer this question: sample size and stationarity. The precise measurements of these two metrics will be the primary focus of Chapter 4, but for now we will take a moment to lay the groundwork for where we are headed. Let's take a look at sample size first.

Sample size is the number of observations that are in the measured return distribution. If the number of observations is small, there is no way the true distribution of the asset can be measured. On the flipside, if the number of measurements is large enough, we actually have a shot at reconstructing the true distribution. An extreme example brings this point home. If I told you I measured the Standard & Poor's (S&P) 500 return for two months and was going to assume that all months for the next 10 years behaved similar to those two measured months, you would call me crazy, and rightfully so, given that my sample size is comically small. In Chapter 4 we will introduce precise criteria that inform us whether our sample size is sufficient to create a reasonable measure of the true distribution.

When we know for sure that there are not enough observations to accurately reconstruct the true distribution (i.e. our sample size is limited for one reason or another), there are a number of interesting techniques that try to assist the forecaster by introducing structure (and approximation error) to help ground the problem in reality. There are 2 main classes of estimators besides the non-parametric type: maximum likelihood and shrinkage. We will not be focusing on these other estimation methods in this book, but it is valuable to take a quick digression on these tools to understand why we avoid them.

For the class of estimators that assume a certain distribution—so-called maximum likelihood estimators—we are forcing our joint return distribution to have the characteristics of the assumed distribution and then estimating the parameters that define that distribution. By virtue of enforcing a certain return distribution on our underlying process, we have minimized the effective number of parameters we need to estimate relative to the full estimation problem. A popular example would be to assume that financial assets individually follow a Pareto distribution and interact via a t copula, which together would help capture non-normal and non-linear behavior; but this method also introduces additional mathematical complexity and forces our assets to have very particular behaviors that may not exactly represent reality. I mentioned earlier that there is a beauty and simplicity in using the entire distribution for our EU problem: we capture infinite moments of complexity purely via the joint return distributions without introducing any (complicated) assumptions. Yes, this comes at the cost of a more challenging estimation problem, but when possible, we would rather tackle that challenge than introduce complexity while simultaneously enforcing artificial constraints that introduce approximation error.[22]

For the class of estimators deployed when even less data is available—so-called shrinkage estimators—more robust estimates come at the cost of incorporating data that is not associated with the true return distribution in any way. One of the most famous shrinkage estimators is the Black–Litterman model, which combines an advisor's return estimates with the market portfolio's implied returns.[23] Unfortunately, this tool suddenly has your estimate closely tied to another estimate: the market portfolio's implied returns. But who is to say this is a useful metric? In reality you are actually starting to manage your portfolio to a benchmark, in this instance the global cap-weighted benchmark. I agree that if you have very little forecasting information, this is indeed a potentially viable starting point, considering its incorporation of the wisdom of the market. But unless we are in that extreme situation of having very little distribution information, we should be avoiding this tool, given the long list of assumptions (how different investors model markets, how liquidity needs affect their allocations, how taxes affect their allocations, etc.) one needs to make to get to the market's implied returns, which each introduce their own approximation and estimation error. While most shrinkage estimators

---

[22]Full disclosure: in the current setting I am more concerned with keeping things simple than with the approximation error that is typically introduced by presupposing the shape of joint return distributions. These forced distributional patterns can indeed be very helpful and precise, and I steer clear of them mostly to continue down the more intuitive path of deploying historical distributions within an advisory framework.

[23]The market portfolio's implied returns are the returns found by taking the market caps of all asset classes and reverse-optimizing them to find the returns expected by investors based on the assumption that all investors on the planet ran a mean-variance optimization to find their portfolio weights.

are generally less mathematically complex than maximum likelihood estimators, this class of estimators often leave me feeling like you're just adding a ton of other approximation and estimation errors to your process, which is the primary reason we would like to avoid them.

Attilio Meucci, one of the world's leading researchers in forecasting financial markets, has a wonderful graphic on the subject of sample size and estimation techniques that has been reprinted in Figure 1.6 (Meucci, ARPM Lab – www.arpm.co). As you can see, if your sample size T is large enough, the optimal estimator is non-parametric, shown on the graphic as having the lowest estimation error among the three types of estimators. In Chapter 4, we review techniques for assessing whether your sample size is large enough to utilize historical data as a primary source of forecasts. But I ultimately view the non-parametric estimation of the return distribution as being so much simpler than other methods, that we have little choice but to deploy the pure historical estimation for any practical advisor framework, to the extent that I would even be comfortable deploying this methodology with sample sizes in the middle of Figure 1.6 that could conceivably benefit from other estimation techniques. As is done throughout the book, and outlined in the preface, the framework laid out here always seeks the most optimal and accurate solution while simultaneously bringing to bear a practical solution. It is precisely in that vein that I advocate non-parametric estimation as our core solution to minimizing estimation error.

Assuming we have a sufficiently large sample size to deploy historical estimates as forecasts, how do we know our non-parametric estimate is

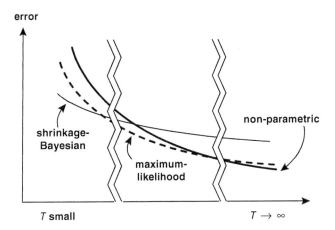

FIGURE 1.6 Estimation Error vs. Sample Size T (Reprinted with Permission from A. Meucci – ARPM Lab – www.arpm.co)

actually a good forecast of the future? In other words, how do we know that history will repeat itself? We need to break this question up into two parts: (1) How do we know a return source repeats without any systematic deviations we could exploit? and (2) How do we know a return source won't suddenly and irreversibly change for the long haul?

History repeating in the context of return distributions amounts to asking the question of whether the return distribution changes over time. Admittedly, we know that many assets both trend over short horizons and revert to the mean over intermediate term horizons; so we know over these horizons that history indeed does not simply repeat itself. But in the preface we made three assumptions, the first of which was that we were only interested in managing portfolios over long horizons. Therefore, the question of history repeating for our purposes is only relevant over multi-decade periods, which will generally hold for investable assets.

A distribution that is the same in one period of time as another period of time is formally called stationary. To test for stationarity we will provide a tool for comparing two return distributions to see whether they are similar enough to conclude that they are statistically the same. We will then use this tool to compare the return distribution from one multi-decade period to the next multi-decade period, to see if history indeed repeats itself. And in that process we will also provide the means to account for secular shifts over long-term horizons from effects like interest rate regime shifts.

At this point we still haven't addressed the question of sudden and irreversible changes to a return source that would make history irrelevant. Unfortunately we will not explicitly address this topic here, as it is beyond the scope of this book. Implicitly, though, by following the framework outlined in Chapter 3—which focuses on asset classes that have well-defined and logical risk premia—the intention is that we are only investing in assets whose return stream is expected to continue. For example, we assume that the compensation human beings demand for investing in companies (AKA the equity risk premium) is an invariant. In this book we always assume that the risk premia we choose to invest in will continue indefinitely.

The main takeaway here is that we will always attack the estimation problem head on and not try to obscure it or avoid it at any stage of our process. By investing in return sources that are stationary, and deploying large sample sizes for healthy measurement, we will be able to confidently utilize forecasts predominantly based on history.

Reducing Sensitivity to Estimation Error

We have just laid out a system for creating a joint return distribution estimate that is sensible (low estimation error) and we are now ready to push this forecast into our optimizer. But how sensitive to estimation error is the EU maximization process? Does the sensitivity preclude us from using models based on estimates that inevitably have errors altogether? And which estimates are the most critical for optimal performance of our portfolio? Are there specific moments we should focus on minimizing estimation error for?

The answer to all these questions is that it depends on the asset classes you are optimizing (Kinlaw, Kritzman, & Turkington, 2017). In general, there are two key takeaways on the topic of optimizer sensitivity to inputs. The first is that portfolios are more sensitive to means than variances (and higher moments) because utility depends linearly on returns but quadratically on variance terms (and cubically on skew, quadratically on kurtosis, etc.), as outlined by Eq. (1.4). Therefore, we need to ensure that our distribution estimate is completely buttoned up at the mean estimation level, by way of a large sample size, and then slowly relax the error bar requirements of our sampled distribution as we consider higher moments. While we are not directly estimating the mean or any higher moments in our process of estimating the entire return distribution, we are certainly implicitly doing so. Hence, in the process of estimating the entire return distribution, we will need to assess the accuracy of each moment estimate embedded in our full distribution estimate, and ensure our error bars are sufficient on a moment-by-moment basis. This issue will be fully covered in Chapter 4, alongside the rest of our discussion on sample size.

The second key takeaway on sensitivity to estimation error is that highly correlated assets generate much more input sensitivity in optimizers than less correlated assets. The return sensitivity seen in Figure 1.5 was largely attributable to the fact that large cap and small cap equities are highly correlated. Chapter 3 will address this sensitivity issue, where comovement effects are minimized by shrinking the universe of investments to the minimal set of orthogonal assets that still respects our client's utility function and their desired risk factor exposures. Note the careful use of "comovement" in the last sentence rather than covariance or correlation. The joint return distribution that is input into our optimizer considers not only linear comovements (covariance) but higher order comovements (coskewness, cokurtosis, etc.) as well. The method we review in Chapter 3 helps reduce sensitivity due to comovement, although it is greatly driven by linear comovement since it's a second order effect (as opposed to third or higher). Since the method includes higher order comovements as well, we must carefully shift to the more generalized terminology of comovement in that context.

Before we wrap up our discussion on the sensitivity to estimation error, let me make two quick points. First, there are a lot of solutions out there that address the error sensitivity problem by completely avoiding it. For example, the 60/40 prescription always allocates 60% to US equities and 40% to US bonds; while the 1/N portfolio equally invests in N assets. We will not consider these "heuristic" models for our clients, as they have zero connection with client utility or asset behavior. Second, there are a number of solutions that try to smooth the sensitivity to estimation error algorithmically, such as portfolio resampling, the Black–Litterman model,[24] or robust optimization; but these models come at the cost of creating suboptimal portfolios,[25] as they generally ignore higher moments and introduce mathematical complexities not suitable for an advisory practice. In this book we will solely look to address optimizer sensitivity to estimation error by tackling it head on with statistically sound sampling from history and avoidance of non-orthogonal assets.

A MODERN DEFINITION OF ASSET ALLOCATION

It should be clear at this point that asset allocation should be defined as the process of *maximizing a client's expected utility while minimizing the effects of estimation error.* One should clearly not maximize utility with poor inputs, as the outputs to the process will not be relevant to future realizations of capital markets. At the other extreme, one should not accept a model that minimizes estimation error at the expense of ignoring client utility details or real-world asset behavior.

Hopefully, I have also substantiated the more explicit approach of maximizing a utility function with *not one but three* dimensions of client risk preferences while minimizing estimation error and its consequences by only investing in *distinct assets* and using *statistically sound historical estimates* as a forecast starting point.

This approach has a couple of key ramifications I want to reiterate briefly. First, we are completely committed to specifying each client's utility function, fully avoiding any approximation error at the problem specification stage. Specifying a utility function is not a common practice today, but with the right tools and a little training, it will provide an accurate and actionable assessment of risk preferences while providing advisors with a powerful framework with which to engage clients.

---

[24]The Black–Litterman model was also showcased earlier as a shrinkage estimator. It is on this list as well because it additionally has features that help with the sensitivity of the optimizer.

[25]Each model introduces some form of approximation error to address the optimizer's sensitivity to inputs, similar to the way maximum likelihood and shrinkage estimators introduced approximation error to help improve estimation error.

Second, the maximization of the full utility function requires returns-based optimization, where a forecast of all possible joint returns across assets is needed. This requirement moves us away from forecasting asset return moments, such as mean and variance, and into the business of forecasting the entire joint return distribution, which is just a long series of possible monthly returns for each asset. And it forces us to leverage historical data as much as possible, given the tremendously specific return outcomes required.

Third, estimation error and its consequences are addressed non-parametrically. This approach avoids any approximation error during forecasting and tremendously simplifies the estimation process for advisors. But it requires careful retort by users as to the statistical quality of the estimates (sample size) and the reasonableness of the assumption that history will repeat itself (stationarity). Additionally, advisors will dogmatically have to avoid any assets that do not qualify as orthogonal—a challenging responsibility in the world of asset proliferation and the desire to present a client with perceived value via complexity.

The remainder of this book will help advisors set up the process laid out in this section in a systematic and intuitive way. The process is certainly more intricate than other sub-optimal approaches, but my hope is that this optimal framework will ultimately be very accurate and intuitive to both advisors and their clients.

Let's now jump into step 1 of the four-step framework just laid out: setting the client risk profile.

2

The Client Risk Profile

In this chapter we take the first of four steps on our journey to finding a client's optimal asset allocation: setting the client's risk profile. The chapter begins with the careful measurement of client preferences regarding risk aversion, loss aversion, and reflection. Standard of living risk is then analyzed via a simple balance sheet model to help decide whether risk aversion and our two behavioral biases, loss aversion and reflection, should be moderated in order to meet the long-term goals of the portfolio. These two steps in conjunction will help fully specify our clients' utility function in a systematic and precise way.

Key Takeaways:

1. All three utility function parameters are measured via lottery-based questionnaires, departing from the traditional qualitative question-naires for risk assessment.
2. Standard of living risk is introduced as a simple method for turning our single-period problem into a multi-period problem, and is the key metric used for systematically moderating or accommodating risk aversion, loss aversion, and reflection in order to meet long-term goals.
3. The discretionary wealth ascertained from a client balance sheet is a natural measure for standard of living risk and systematically solves the glidepath problem in a concise and personalized manner.

INTRODUCTION

The simplest and most popular approach to establishing a client-specific risk profile is to measure volatility aversion by posing a series of qualitative questions on topics such as self-assessment of risk tolerance, experience with risk, passion for gambling, and time to retirement, and then using that score to choose a portfolio along the mean-variance efficient frontier at a risk level commensurate with the score. Unfortunately, there are three major issues with this process from the vantage point of this book. First, the typical risk tolerance questionnaire has a number of qualitative questions that are trying to pinpoint a very numerical quantity (utility second derivative), without a well-substantiated mapping from qualitative to quantitative.[1] Second, the goals of the client are often analyzed qualitatively within the risk tolerance questions, without formal connection to well-defined retirement or multi-generational goals. And, third, this process has only been built to find a single parameter, uninteresting to us given our utility function that requires specification of three distinct risk preferences.

To address these issues, a concise two-step process is introduced. First, we present three lottery-style questionnaires, which precisely specify our clients' risk aversion, loss aversion, and reflection. We abandon the standard qualitative battery of questions, which convolutes different types of risk preferences and lacks a solid theoretical basis for mapping to utility parameters, in favor of our more numerate and surgical approach. Second, we deploy a simple balance sheet model to measure standard of living risk, which informs whether risk preferences need to be moderated in order to meet the client's goals. This model precisely accounts for standard lifecycle concepts, such as time horizon and savings rate, in a hyper-personalized manner while allowing us to avoid more complicated multi-period solutions.

MEASURING PREFERENCES

Risk Aversion

We begin specification of our three-dimensional risk profile utility function (Eq. (1.8)) by measuring risk aversion γ, the neoclassical utility parameter that sets the second derivative of our utility function (AKA preference to volatility) if there is no loss aversion or reflection. To set this parameter systematically, we deploy a lottery-style questionnaire (Holt & Laury, 2002). Each question presents a simple binary gambling choice where you must choose between two options. Figure 2.1 shows a simple five-question version of this type of questionnaire that is explicitly designed to measure risk aversion. Each question poses a gamble to the client that, when aggregated together, can precisely determine the curvature of a power utility function. Preferences for the sure bet, which has a lower expected payout, map to a higher curvature utility function (more negative second derivative) and hence

---

[1]These questionnaires also calculate the aversion to volatility by a simple tally of answers, which as you will see in Chapter 5, could lead to assessments that are way off from reality due to nuances of our three-dimensional utility function.

Question 1: Between the following two options, which do you prefer?
　　　　　Choice A: 50% chance to win $2.00, 50% chance to win $1.60.
　　　　　Choice B: 50% chance to win $3.85, 50% chance to win $0.10.
Question 2: Between the following two options, which do you prefer?
　　　　　Choice A: 60% chance to win $2.00, 40% chance to win $1.60.
　　　　　Choice B: 60% chance to win $3.85, 40% chance to win $0.10.
Question 3: Between the following two options, which do you prefer?
　　　　　Choice A: 70% chance to win $2.00, 30% chance to win $1.60.
　　　　　Choice B: 70% chance to win $3.85, 30% chance to win $0.10.
Question 4: Between the following two options, which do you prefer?
　　　　　Choice A: 80% chance to win $2.00, 20% chance to win $1.60.
　　　　　Choice B: 80% chance to win $3.85, 20% chance to win $0.10.
Question 5: Between the following two options, which do you prefer?
　　　　　Choice A: 90% chance to win $2.00, 10% chance to win $1.60.
　　　　　Choice B: 90% chance to win $3.85, 10% chance to win $0.10.

FIGURE 2.1　Risk Aversion Questionnaire

higher risk aversion while preferences to bigger payouts that are less certain map to a utility function with less curvature (less negative second derivative, noting that a straight line would have zero second derivative) and hence lower risk aversion. Note that these questions are explicitly written as a single gamble, not an opportunity to make the gamble repeatedly hundreds or thousands of times. This one-time phrasing aligns with the natural disposition for investors to be myopic (allowing short-term performance to influence their ability to stick with a long-term investment plan), as well our single-period representation of the portfolio decision problem as outlined in the preface.[2]

But how do the questions in Figure 2.1 help assign a precise risk aversion to a client? Seeing where a client decides to begin choosing Choice B allows us to set the risk aversion. If a client chooses Choice B for every question, they are clearly displaying little risk aversion. Clients who choose Choice A until question 4 or 5 are clearly more risk averse. Risk aversion is

---

[2]The single gamble phrasing also helps completely avoid the additional complexities of how individuals make decisions regarding repeated gambles versus single gambles, a famous paradox dubbed the "fallacy of large numbers" by Paul Samuelson (Samuelson, 1963), which actually varies based on investor sophistication (Benartzi & Thaler, 1999).

	Client 1	Client 2	Client 3	Client 4	Client 5	Client 6
Question 1	Choice A	Choice A	Choice A	Choice A	Choice A	Choice B
Question 2	Choice A	Choice A	Choice A	Choice A	Choice B	Choice B
Question 3	Choice A	Choice A	Choice A	Choice B	Choice B	Choice B
Question 4	Choice A	Choice A	Choice B	Choice B	Choice B	Choice B
Question 5	Choice A	Choice B	Choice B	Choice B	Choice B	Choice B
γ Assignment:	12	7	4.5	3	2	1.5
Percent of Population:	2.5%	2.5%	10%	25%	15%	45%
Percent of Population: (real & 20x gambles)	5%	10%	20%	25%	20%	20%

FIGURE 2.2   Risk Aversion Mapping

parameterized here between 1.5 and 12, as laid out in Figure 2.2.[3] We show the percentage of the population that advisors can expect in each bucket based on these questions. In addition, Figure 2.2 shows the percentage of the population we would expect in each bucket if we multiplied the gamble sizes in our lottery questionnaire by 20 and actually paid out winnings. As you might expect, risk aversion shifts significantly higher when the gambles are real and 20 times greater in magnitude (these are known as "incentive effects") (Holt & Laury, 2002). So, yes, we are now in a pickle. I have provided a small gamble lottery questionnaire that is completely hypothetical, which really doesn't elicit accurate subjective risk aversion results. And it turns out that it is not the 1x to 20x change or the hypothetical to real change that is responsible for this shift in risk aversion: it is the combination! I have never come across a wealth manager who elicits risk preferences with real gambling situations; but empirical testing has definitively shown us that this is the only way to measure true preferences.

What about the other possible permutations of answers besides the five shown in Figure 2.2? It has been shown that over 90% of respondents will be "consistent" and answer these questions monotonically, meaning once they flip their answer it will stay flipped. For those clients who do not answer in that way, it is useful for the advisor to insert herself and

---

[3]We parameterize this way by combining two perspectives on this topic: (1) the non-linear representation of risk aversion captured by the precise lottery questions being deployed in Figure 2.1 (Holt & Laury, 2002); and (2) a range of risk aversions that provides significant variance in the context of financial decision-making (Ang, 2014).

review the questionnaire with the client as an educational exercise. From a programmatic standpoint, my software utilizes the lowest question number where B is chosen to set γ (if B is never chosen, then risk aversion is set to 12) regardless of answers to higher question numbers. This approach sidesteps the monotonicity question, but still allows a client to answer non-monotonically. One could also tackle this issue programmatically by locking the answer choices to always be monotonic. For example, if someone chooses B for question 3, then questions 4 and 5 are automatically set to B; but then you would lose the additional color of a client misunderstanding the question as discussed above.

In this section I have completely moved away from the style of risk questionnaire that has become popular over the past decade. Those questionnaires measure risk preferences in a number of different ways (self-assessment of risk tolerance, experience with risk, etc.) and in a more qualitative format than the gambling questions I have deployed here. Such a question might have a client rate their comfort level with risk among four choices (low, medium, high, very high). While there is indeed interesting research that explores the value of more qualitative and multi-dimensional questionnaires (Grable & Lytton, 1999) and of tying them explicitly to individual preferences or biases (Guillemette, Yao, & James, 2015), I have opted to pursue the more quantitative questionnaire path. My motivation to take this route is twofold.

First, I will always prefer a test that precisely maps to the thing we are trying to measure. In the academic world of questionnaire design, a test's ability to measure the intended feature is known as "validity" (Grable, 2017). Validity is generally tough to measure since we are typically trying to assess a quantity with no right answer we can compare to. Say you were creating an incredibly cheap clock and you wanted to make sure it was accurate. In that case, you have a great benchmark to test for validity: the National Institute of Standards and Technology (NIST) atomic clock.[4] But in the case of risk preference assessments we have no such benchmark. What we do have is a precise definition of these parameters from our utility function, from which we can reverse engineer a series of questions that can help precisely measure the parameter. By performing

---

[4]I take significant exception with the way validity is often tested in this space, hence my strong desire to avoid the issue by construction rather than by measurement. As an example, the Survey of Consumer Finance (SCF) risk assessment item was used by Grable and Lytton (Grable & Lytton, 1999) to study the validity of their famous 13-item questionnaire by looking at the correlation between their score and the SCF assessment. But in their work they also write that, "The SCF risk assessment item has been widely used as a proxy for financial risk tolerance, although no published documentation exists to substantiate the validity of this item."

this reverse engineering of the questions from the utility function, the hope is that we have near 100% validity (at least theoretically if a robot were answering it[5]).

You may be concerned at this point that we have traded improved validity for more challenging mathematical questions. It has been my experience that for most clients these more mathematical questions are quite straightforward, and they precisely elicit the emotional, gut reactions we are looking to ascertain in the process. Actually, it is usually the advisors who struggle more with these questions as they may view the questionnaires as more of a test, which inevitably leads them to wonder whether they should make decisions based less on the emotional nature of risk aversion and more on expected value. While this behavior is less frequent in clients, it will certainly come up for more financially literate clients, and advisors should be prepared to recognize this rabbit hole situation and steer clients toward a more emotional response to the questions. Ultimately, I am very hopeful that these more quantitative diagnostic questions will represent a welcome component to the advisor's engagement with the client while preserving the precision of what we are trying to achieve.

Second, the simplest path for me to take in diagnosing both loss aversion and reflection was through lottery-style questions similar to those presented here for risk aversion. In an effort to stay consistent with the style of questionnaire deployed for setting all three utility features, I then had to stick with lottery-style for the risk aversion feature. At the end of the day, as long as a risk parameter questionnaire is rigorously tested for validity, and the limits of the test are well understood by the advisor, I believe the exact style of the questionnaire is flexible and can be guided by the real-world usage.

Before we move on from risk aversion, let me briefly mention that it has been shown that risk aversion changes in time for investors: they are more risk-averse after losses ("break-even effect") and less risk-averse after wins ("house money effect") (Thaler & Johnson, 1990).[6] It is thus very useful for an advisor to periodically measure their client's risk aversion to account for this effect, and to educate their client on the topic (the same periodic check-in should be done for loss aversion and reflection as well). But which risk aversion do you deploy if you're regularly measuring it and it is changing

---

[5] Clients may misinterpret questions or have temporary personal influences that prevent this from being a 100% valid construction, which has to do with the "reliability" of the test, a subset of validity that we will come back to shortly.

[6] Fun fact: time-varying risk aversion helps explain the "equity premium puzzle" (Campbell & Cochrane, 1999), whereby economists were unable to justify the magnitude of the historically observed equity risk premium using a standard consumption-based asset pricing model. The updated model deploys a time-varying, habit-based utility to rectify theory with empirical findings.

in time? You want to use the level that is established during average market environments, avoiding the break-even and house money effects altogether. Both of these effects are due to the component of prospect theory that we have ignored (see "decision weights" in footnote 17 of Chapter 1), and as such, we do not want to unwittingly introduce it into our process.

Loss Aversion

In Chapter 1 we showed that the first behavioral deviation from neoclassical utility we want to consider is loss aversion, coded into client risk preferences by assigning a value for λ in our utility function (Eq. (1.8)) that deviates from 1. This parameter ascertains an irrational asymmetric discomfort of downside versus upside moves, greatly influencing portfolio preferences regarding drawdowns. To precisely assess one's degree of loss aversion, we will continue to deploy lottery-style gambling questions (Gachter, Johnson, & Herrmann, 2007). Such a question for loss aversion might ask: Would you accept or reject a lottery where a coin is flipped and the payout is −$1 when tails comes up and +$2 when heads comes up? If you say no to this, then we can conclude you have some degree of loss aversion. Why is that so? First, the question refers to both losses and gains, stepping us away from the arena of risk aversion where all possible outcomes were gains, and into the world of loss aversion which measures our preferences for gains versus losses. Second, we are avoiding the background curvature given by our utility function's risk aversion by only considering bets that are small enough to ensure that the utility function is effectively linear between the two outcomes[7]—which turns the problem into a pure expected return problem (which any rational investor would accept in this specific instance). Hence, if you reject this particular lottery, you are showcasing a bias to loss aversion. But how do we take a short list of questions like the one above and turn them into a score?

For precise score measurement we will again deploy a sequence of lottery questions, which directly implies a loss aversion score when analyzed as a whole. Figure 2.3 outlines four questions that follow a simple sequence of increasingly risky bets. The basic idea here is similar to what we just deployed to measure risk aversion, except now losses are involved: each lottery has larger losses as we go down the list, and the point at which someone begins to reject the lottery pinpoints their loss aversion precisely. The earlier in this sequence of gambles that a client begins to reject the lottery, the

---

[7]This then informs us that the dollar amount in our risk aversion questions wasn't large enough to diagnose the non-linearity. We will address this issue, along with other gamble sizing issues, after we review our reflection questionnaire.

Question 1: A fair coin is flipped. Heads you lose $3, tails you win $6.

> **Choice A:** Accept the lottery.
> **Choice B:** Reject the lottery.

Question 2: A fair coin is flipped. Heads you lose $4, tails you win $6.

> **Choice A:** Accept the lottery.
> **Choice B:** Reject the lottery.

Question 3: A fair coin is flipped. Heads you lose $5, tails you win $6.

> **Choice A:** Accept the lottery.
> **Choice B:** Reject the lottery.

Question 4: A fair coin is flipped. Heads you lose $6, tails you win $6.

> **Choice A:** Accept the lottery.
> **Choice B:** Reject the lottery.

FIGURE 2.3 Loss Aversion Questionnaire

more loss averse they are, given that all bets are completely rational from an expected utility standpoint: they are all just expected value decisions, as reviewed in the previous paragraph.

For the remainder of this book, λ is parameterized between 1 (no loss aversion) and 3 (maximal loss aversion), aligning with modern research on the subject that shows clients often have loss aversion between these levels (Gachter, Johnson, & Herrmann, 2007). The exact mapping from lottery rejection point to λ is laid out in Figure 2.4. As you can see, λ is just the ratio of win versus loss magnitudes where the questionnaire is last accepted—a 100% valid mapping of questionnaire to preference that is much more transparent than the mapping for risk aversion (which requires additional utility mathematics). Figure 2.4 also shows expectations for how clients should roughly be distributed across the bins.[8]

Finally, similar to the risk aversion questionnaire, around 90% of respondents will answer monotonically (i.e. once the client flips to Choice B they will continue to do so for the rest of the questions). Similar to what

---

[8] A few comments. (1) Many studies cite slightly higher mean loss aversions (2 vs. 1.6 in our setup), but this seems to be due to an inappropriate focus on the riskless version of these lottery questionnaires (Gachter, Johnson, & Herrmann, 2007). (2) There are indeed individuals with $\lambda < 1$, but we do not allow for that and just bin that population in the $\lambda = 1$ camp (Gachter, Johnson, & Herrmann, 2007). (3) I parameterize 3 as the max λ based on the fact that just about everyone in the world would accept the subsequent lottery of $2 vs. $6 that would be the next question at the top of the questionnaire (Gachter, Johnson, & Herrmann, 2007).

	Client 1	Client 2	Client 3	Client 4	Client 5
Question 1	Accept	Accept	Accept	Accept	Reject
Question 2	Accept	Accept	Accept	Reject	Reject
Question 3	Accept	Accept	Reject	Reject	Reject
Question 4	Accept	Reject	Reject	Reject	Reject
λ Assignment:	1	1.2	1.5	2	3
Percent of Population:	30%	20%	25%	15%	10%

FIGURE 2.4　Loss Aversion Mapping

we did for risk aversion, my software utilizes the lowest question number that is rejected to set λ, regardless of answers to higher question numbers, hence sidestepping the monotonicity question.

Reflection

The second deviation from a purely rational utility function we need to assess is reflection. As a reminder, this feature is captured by our three-dimensional risk profile utility function (Eq. (1.8)) via the specification of reflection φ that departs from 0, informing us that a client has an irrational preference to become risk-seeking when contemplating losing positions. But in contrast to risk aversion and loss aversion, which are captured by variable parameters in our utility function, reflection is a binary variable that can only take on the value 0 or 1. As mentioned in Chapter 1, we could have parameterized reflection further by setting the curvature of the S-shaped function differently in the domains of losses and gains. But to help facilitate an intuitive interpretation of our utility function that translates well to clients, we have opted to keep things simple and just flag reflection as existing or not.

So how do we diagnose reflection in our clients? For this we utilize the question set shown in Figure 2.5, which asks the exact same question twice, once in the gain domain and once in the loss domain.[9] There are four possible combinations of answers a client can choose during this questionnaire: Choices A and 1, Choices A and 2, Choices B and 1, and Choices B and 2. The only combination set of the four that indicates

---

[9]This setup looks similar to the typical questionnaire used to diagnose the framing effect, but I must emphasize that these are completely different effects (Fagley, 1993). Reflection refers to having opposite risk preferences for gains and losses while framing refers to having different risk preferences for the same gamble, depending on how the gamble is propositioned.

Question 1: Between the following two options, which do you prefer?

        Choice A: A certain gain of $20.

        Choice B: A 1/3 chance of gaining $60.

Question 2: Between the following two options, which do you prefer?

        Choice 1: A certain loss of $20.

        Choice 2: A 1/3 chance of losing $60.

FIGURE 2.5   Reflection Questionnaire

reflection ($\varphi = 1$) is the second (Choices A and 2), as we see the client opting for the risk-averse option in the gain domain and the risk-seeking option in the loss domain. None of the other three answer combinations would be consistent with reflection. Hence, we say a client showcases reflection if and only if Choices A and 2 are chosen by the client. In terms of expectations of our clients for reflection, we expect about half of them to be flagged for the reflection bias (Baucells & Villasis, 2010).

Many readers might wonder at this point whether the question set in Figure 2.5, which only contains two questions, is sufficient to diagnose a client's reflection. This is an excellent question; it is essentially asking what the measurement error is for each of the four answer combinations (it is the number of distinct answers that matters more than the number of questions, in terms of diagnostic accuracy). And the same exact question must be asked regarding our risk and loss aversion questionnaires (six and five distinct answers, respectively). We are now entering the domain of questionnaire "reliability" (Grable, 2017).

Besides validity, reliability is the other key requirement of a healthy questionnaire, as it measures how repeatable the results are for a given individual. In other words, it measures the inverse of the questionnaire's measurement error. Said another way, validity measures systematic deviations for every participant in the test, whereas reliability measures the variance around individual respondent answers. An easy way to remember the difference between these two concepts is by thinking of a linear regression from Stats 101, where we always assume the data points we are regressing are perfectly measured (there are no error bars on the data points themselves, AKA reliability is 1), and we analyze whether a linear model is a good representation of our data (i.e. is valid) via R^2 (which runs from 0 to 1).

We can also gain a little more clarity on reliability if we understand how it is measured. There are many ways to do this, but one popular method is to ask the same question to the same person at different points in time and look at the correlation of the answers (i.e. a "test-retest" reliability procedure). A correlation of 1 indicates perfect reliability. Although reliability of questionnaires is of paramount importance, the topic is generally considered to be outside the purview of this book, as it is an entire field in and of itself.

For now I simply assume perfect reliability for our questionnaires since we have four or more distinct answers for each questionnaire (and not just one or two, which would worry me more).

Lottery Question Sizing

We have presented three lottery-style questionnaires designed to measure each utility function parameter accurately. As briefly reviewed for risk aversion, empirical work has shown that the sizing of the questions has a big impact on the responses, where smaller gambles will generally elicit lower risk aversion. Additionally, we saw that loss aversion questions need to be posed with very small gambles. So how do we size all these questions appropriately? There are three key issues at work when sizing the gambles.

The first is that loss aversion is a concept that must be carefully measured without any influence from the curvature of the utility function. Hence, loss aversion gambles should be sized significantly smaller than the risk aversion or reflection questions, which are both squarely related to curvature of utility. The second key constraint is that the loss aversion question must have gamble sizes that are meaningful enough for a client to take the question seriously. If you ask someone worth $50 million about winning or losing a single dollar, the question may be treated the same as if they were gambling with dirt, with zero connection to their true emotional preference. Finally, the risk aversion and reflection questions should be sizable enough to actually measure utility curvature (the opposite situation we are in for loss aversion), and in agreement with the earlier results showing that smaller gambles in risk aversion questions will not elicit true preferences.

To facilitate all three effects one could base the gamble size in the risk aversion and reflection questions on a client's annual income, and then appropriately scale down the loss aversion gamble sizes from there, but not too much. In my software I test clients with risk aversion and reflection gambles that are $1/200^{th}$ of annual income while I deploy loss aversion gambles that are 10 times smaller than that. For example, a client with annual income of $200,000 would answer risk aversion and reflection questions in the $1,000 ballpark while answering questions on loss aversion near $100, an intuitively reasonable solution to our three priorities regarding gamble sizes.

INCORPORATING GOALS

Preference Moderation via SLR

Now that we have measured the three preferences embedded in our client's utility function, are we finished specifying our client's risk profile? Not exactly. It turns out that if you account for the goals of the portfolio, you are naturally confronted with the fact that you may need to moderate (i.e. override) the three parameters of the utility function we have carefully measured.

Up to this point in the book we have deployed assumptions that allow us to focus on the single period portfolio problem of maximizing the following month's expected utility. In addition, we have completely ignored any long-term goals of the portfolio that would require a multi-period framework. But we know our clients indeed have goals for their portfolios. For most of us the goal is to have enough wealth to survive during retirement. For wealthier individuals the goal might be a sizable inheritance for their children. So how do we incorporate goals into our process in a systematic way while still being able to focus on the simplified single-period expected utility problem?

The key here is to realize the following: when we introduce goals, risk taking changes from being a personal preference to a luxury that we may or may not be able to afford. In other words, low risk aversion may need to be moderated if our client's balance sheet isn't able to take on a lot of risk when considering their goals.[10] An extreme example would be a client whose goal is to withdraw tomorrow $100,000 from an account that is currently worth that amount today. Clearly, this client cannot put any risk in the portfolio, or they jeopardize meeting their goal if the portfolio has a down day. Hence, if the portfolio goal is risky but the client has low risk aversion, the preference for risk aversion must be moderated upwards. In effect, if we have a goal in mind that we want executed with certainty, we must start off with a risk-free portfolio, and only if our goals are easily achievable can we then take on more risk. Said another way, risk is a luxury.

What about the financial plan that "gets" a client to lofty financial goals with markedly less than 100% certainty? If your goal is flexible, then yes, you can set out a goal that may not be achieved which can then be updated after failure, but in this book we will be focused on the hyper-fiduciary mission of building portfolios with inflexible goals. We will return to this topic when we discuss Monte Carlo simulations of future expected wealth and how these tools can help us add some flexibility to the plan as long as risk preferences are respected and there is some flexibility in goals. With that said, this book generally recommends the more risk-controlled, goal-focused process that assumes that financial goals are first-and-foremost inflexible, and

---

[10]We assume no opposite version of this, where a high risk aversion needs to be lowered. High risk aversion is considered an immutable limit our client has that is non-negotiable. This assumption formally removes the concept of lowering risk aversion to achieve a goal from our quiver of arrows.

that risk should only be deployed in portfolios when one can sufficiently meet their goals with certainty (i.e. without risky investments).

We will refer to the riskiness of meeting one's portfolio goals as standard of living risk (SLR) (CFA Institute, 2018). One may loosely think of SLR as an inverse measure of the probability of meeting your goals, where lower SLR represents higher probability of meeting your goals and higher SLR represents lower probability of meeting your goals. When SLR is high, as it was in our $100,000 example above, risk aversion will need to be moderated upwards. When SLR is low, we will let the client's natural risk aversion dictate the riskiness of the portfolio.

Many of you will have heard of the term *risk capacity*, a measure of how much risk your goals can handle. If you have, you may also have heard that you don't want your client's risk tolerance (1/risk aversion) to be higher than their risk capacity. This is the exact same system we are discussing here, except this nomenclature inverts the scales of the risk parameters we deploy (SLR is proportional to 1/risk capacity). You may have also seen the phrasing "subjective versus objective risk aversion," where subjective risk aversion is the client preference and objective risk aversion is proportional to 1/risk capacity—where one always wants to ensure the client's portfolio is deployed using the higher of the subjective and objective risk aversion scores.[11] This is the same framework we have put forth here on moderating risk, just with modified lingo that we will deploy within this book when useful.

What about our two behavioral parameters? The same simple concept applies to behavioral biases as well but from a slightly different perspective. The two behavioral preferences we encapsulate in our utility function are both suboptimal when it comes to long-term wealth optimization, and hence are a form of luxury that isn't available to someone who is not likely to meet their goals. Hence, we will moderate both loss aversion and reflection when SLR is high—not because we are taking on too much risk, but rather because we can't afford any sub-optimality. The situation for behavioral biases is even more subtle than that and is worth a short digression.

Moderation of behavioral biases can be conveniently summarized by the framework shown in Figure 2.6.[12]

---

[11]As discussed in Chapter 1, many risk tolerance questionnaires make the mistake of combining subjective and objective risk aversion measures into a single score. Hopefully, we have shown how misleading this can be, since the objective side of the coin shouldn't average with the subjective side; rather, the portfolio should respect the more conservative of the two quantities.

[12]This is a modified version of a concept outlined in a wonderful book by Michael Pompian (Pompian, 2006). I have replaced Pompian's wealth axis with SLR, as there

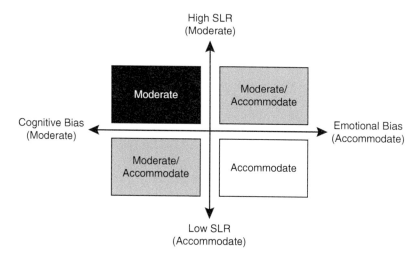

FIGURE 2.6 Moderation vs. Accommodation of Behavioral Biases

Beyond enforcing greater moderation of behavioral biases as SLR increases, the framework also recommends advisors should be less compromising with cognitive biases than they are with emotional biases. The rough idea here is that emotional biases are driven by subconscious responses which are difficult to rectify, which may warrant adaptation to stick with a plan, while cognitive biases are driven by faulty reasoning or a lack of information, which should only be moderated. Why not just tell your client how to behave rationally and that is all?

The premise here is simple: a sub-optimal plan your client can actually follow is better than an optimal plan your client can't follow.[13] In other words, a slightly lower utility portfolio adhered to is better than a portfolio with higher utility that is not adhered to, if your goals can handle such accommodation. A perfect example is the Great Recession. Many clients had portfolios optimized for their risk tolerance, but the portfolio wasn't built with their behavioral biases in mind, and many of these clients got out of the markets at the bottom and didn't reenter until many years later. These

---

may indeed be instances where a wealthy person's goals do not actually allow for accommodation due to the specifics embedded in their balance sheet model. I have also reoriented the direction of the axes.

[13]This is the ideal reason to do this. One can also imagine less altruistic execution, such as an advisor who is looking to keep his job at all costs and to that end creates a portfolio that resonates with the client as much as possible without breaching his fiduciary responsibility, which is certainly not the hope of this system.

clients were much better off in a portfolio that might be sub-optimal for a fully rational investor but one that if adhered to would be much more beneficial than being in cash for extended periods. Fortunately, both components of PT that we account for via our three-dimensional risk profile utility are emotional biases and the two-dimensional framework collapses to a simpler one-dimensional tool that is just a function of SLR; hence, we have the same situation as we do for moderating risk aversion: we will moderate irrational behavioral biases when SLR is high.

What about the litany of other emotional biases that researchers have discovered over the past 50 years (Pompian, 2006)? Why aren't they accounted for in our utility function? It turns out that there are a number of emotional biases that are not relevant for our usage here, or the effect is subsumed by loss aversion and reflection. For example, self-control bias is an important emotional bias tied to one's inability to consume less now for rationally smoothed long-term consumption. While we indeed spend time discussing how the single period problem should be translated into a retirement solution, we assume that self-control bias can be overcome with modern fintech such as automated savings programs.

As another example, consider the endowment bias (a direct consequence of PT), where investors get emotionally tied to individual holdings and have difficulty parting ways with them. In this book we assume clients are not wedded to any positions, by assuming clients have a more distant relationship with their investment portfolios, a trend we only see continuing. Additionally, at the portfolio level the endowment effect is captured by loss aversion, which implies favoring of the status quo (i.e. you won't take a 50/50 bet with equal absolute payoffs).[14] There are many more biases we could cover in this way, but you will just have to trust me that if you first weed out the emotional biases from the cognitive ones, and then remove those biases that don't affect our use case, any biases remaining will be subsumed by reflection and loss aversion.

With the asymmetric view that we will lower risk for a goal but never raise it, and the fact that our two behavioral biases should be moderated as well when goals are lofty due to their sub-optimality, we have hopefully accomplished our intention of the section—to advocate the moderation of all three utility parameters when the goals of the portfolio are increasingly at risk of not being met. In the next section we introduce *discretionary wealth* as a simple yet powerful way to measure SLR. This tool enables us to moderate

---

[14]More mathematically: it has been shown that the correlation between the classic endowment willingness-to-accept (WTA) versus willingness-to-purchase (WTP) test has a 0.64 correlation with the classic loss aversion measure (Gachter, Johnson, & Herrmann, 2007).

our three utility parameters in a systematic yet personalized manner, and ultimately to provide a goals-conscious asset allocation solution.

Discretionary Wealth

To measure SLR we move away from the lottery-based questionnaires and shift to a balance sheet model that can easily capture the client's goals and the risk associated with achieving them. On the left side of the balance sheet is a client's implied assets, which includes both assets currently held and the present value (PV) of all future assets. For our current purposes, we will have only three items on the asset side of the balance sheet: the client's investment portfolio, the value of their home, and the PV of all future savings through employment (i.e. PV of future employment capital minus spending). On the right-hand side of the balance sheet is today's value of all current and future liabilities. In our simple model this will include the client's total current debt (typically school loans and/or a mortgage) and the PV of all expected spending needs during retirement. Figure 2.7 shows the balance sheet model for a client with a $1 million home, a $500k investment portfolio, and a $500k PV of all future savings before retirement. This compares to liabilities of $0 of current debt and a PV of required capital for retirement of $1 million.

So how do we tease SLR out of this model? The key is the client's discretionary wealth (Wilcox, Horvitz, & diBartolomeo, 2006),[15] which is simply

Assets		Liabilities	
Home	$1,000,000	Debt	$0
Investment Portfolio	$500,000	PV (Retirement Capital)	$1,000,000
PV (Employment Capital Less Consumption)	$500,000		

Discretionary Wealth	
Discretionary Wealth = Assets – Liabilities	$1,000,000
SLR = 1– Discretionary Wealth / Total Assets	50%

FIGURE 2.7　Balance Sheet Model

---

[15]The original application of the cited authors' discretionary wealth framework was to use total assets/discretionary wealth as their risk aversion parameter, distinct from our application as an SLR measure used to moderate preferences.

total implied assets minus total implied liabilities—that is, total net implied assets. What is this number exactly and how does it help us? Simply said, discretionary wealth is the wealth you don't need. More precisely, it tells you how much money you have left after all your current and future obligations are met by only investing at the risk-free rate. If discretionary wealth is high, then your assets are ample to meet liabilities and you indeed have the luxury of deploying risk in your portfolio. If it is low, then you have very little padding in your financial situation and you don't have the luxury of taking on much risk. Hence, discretionary wealth is the perfect metric to help us assess whether someone's retirement goals are at risk. In the example given in Figure 2.7 we have discretionary wealth of $1 million, a favorable position for our client, and one that should afford them the luxury to take on risk in their investment portfolio.

Let's now move to formally mapping discretionary wealth to SLR. First let's distinguish two key regimes of discretionary wealth: greater than 0 and less than 0. When discretionary wealth is less than zero, we have a problem. The balance sheet model is telling us that even if we invest in the risk-free asset, our client will not achieve their goals. In this case, the client's balance sheet must be modified via some tough conversations. To move discretionary wealth into positive territory a client can take certain actions such as working longer, increasing their savings, reducing their income level in retirement, and minimizing liabilities.

Once our client is in positive discretionary wealth territory, we note that the ratio of discretionary wealth to total implied assets will always lie between 0% and 100%, which is a great indicator of a client's current financial health. If a client has a 0% ratio of discretionary wealth to total assets, then they are just squeaking by to meet their financial goals and have zero ability to take on risk. On the other extreme of the spectrum, a 100% ratio means the client has zero liabilities relative to assets and can take on as much risk as they would be interested in accepting. To map this ratio to SLR is now simple:

Equation 2.1 Formal Definition of SLR

$$SLR = 100\% - \frac{Discretionary\ Wealth}{Total\ Implied\ Assets}$$

Once discretionary wealth is greater than 0, SLR will always lie between 0 and 100%, a very simple and intuitive range for measuring standard of living risk. In our case study in Figure 2.7 our client's $1 million of discretionary wealth maps to an SLR of 50%, perhaps a slightly less favorable number than you might expect given the impressive absolute level of the discretionary wealth. This outcome highlights that it is not the absolute level of discretionary wealth that matters, but rather the ratio of discretionary wealth to total implied assets, since the health of a certain level of discretionary wealth is irrelevant without a full comprehension of how the discretionary wealth compares to the ultimate liabilities. Even a large discretionary wealth isn't that attractive if the liabilities are incredibly large since one's level of padding is all relative!

The last step of moderating our three utility preferences is to use SLR, as defined by Eq. (2.1), to adjust our risk and behavioral parameters measured by our lottery-style questionnaires. Our SLR will have us maximally moderating at 100% and not moderating at all at 0%, but the precise approach for systematically moderating preferences via SLR will be different for each parameter. Let me note upfront that the precise details for the moderation system presented below is an intuitively reasonable framework, but I am sure it can be improved upon, and I encourage others to put forth more advanced logic around the precise moderation rules.

For risk aversion, we map the SLR scale of 0–100% to a score from 1.5 to 12 and then set our risk aversion parameter to be the greater of the measured risk aversion and this SLR-based "objective" risk aversion. Hence, if a client has plenty of risk tolerance in the form of a risk aversion of 3, but his SLR is 50% (mapping to an objective risk aversion of 6.75), then the γ of our utility function is set to 6.75 (the higher of the two). This moderation rule, along with the rules for loss aversion and reflection that we are about to review, are summarized in Figure 2.8.

To reiterate, when SLR hits 100%, we are moderating to a very low-risk portfolio ($\gamma = 12$ is not completely risk-free, but one could update this system to moderate to a completely risk-free portfolio). By moderating to a minimal-risk portfolio we are effectively guaranteeing that we will meet our liabilities. As described in the beginning of this section, our moderation process is very risk-focused, putting success of financial goals above all else (while respecting any immutable risk aversion).

For loss aversion we will do something similar but now our directionality is flipped. We map SLR to a score from 3 to 1 as SLR moves from

	Measured	Moderated
Risk Aversion	γ	max (γ, 1.5+10.5*SLR)
Loss Aversion	λ	min (λ, 3-2*SLR)
Reflection	φ	if SLR $\geq$ 50% then 0 else φ

FIGURE 2.8 Preference Moderation via SLR

0 to 100%, and we set λ deployed in our utility function as the lower of this SLR-mapped loss aversion number and the measured preference. For instance, if our client has a subjective λ of 3 and an SLR of 50% (mapping to an "objective" λ of 2), we will moderate loss aversion down to the objective score of 2.

Finally, we must moderate those clients that exhibit a reflection bias while having a high SLR. Since reflection for us is not continuous, we must choose an SLR level to discretely moderate our client from an S-shaped utility (φ = 1) to a power or kinked functional form (φ = 0). For the remainder of this book we will assume an SLR of 50% or greater to represent a reasonable level of discretionary assets where reflection should be discretely moderated. In this way we have planted our flag in the sand that SLR of 50% is a reasonable tipping point for us to take the viability of our goals very seriously and begin to completely abandon any suboptimal binary biases. This rule will become better motivated in Chapter 5 when we see how our portfolios evolve as a function of our three parameters, and how moderation of preferences by SLR will impact portfolios.

An interesting question might come up for you at this stage: Should we ever accommodate very extreme cases of behavioral biases even when SLR is near 100%? In theory, one could indeed do this by engaging in the incredibly challenging conversation of lowering SLR down to the 0–25% range by dramatically changing the client's goals. However, given the magnitude of the ask to bring SLR down so significantly, it will in general be a lot more reasonable to moderate the biases while only having to bring SLR to 75% or so.

The purpose of the SLR definition presented here was to provide a succinct and completely systematic tool to moderate three distinct preferences in an effort to achieve given financial goals. This system rested on a strong premise, that financial goals should be paramount and 100% success rates were a driving factor behind the system. Let's now review other tools commonly used when moderating preferences for goals and see how they stack up.

Comparison with Monte Carlo

Many advisors today deploy Monte Carlo simulations to investigate whether goals are likely to be reached. In that setting an advisor analyzes all possible cash flow outcomes over long horizons by running simulations of all possible expected capital market paths. By then looking at the portfolio's success rate, which is the percentage of simulated portfolio paths that achieve the desired cash flow goals, the advisor can then iteratively moderate the recommended asset allocation or goals (or even worse, preferences) until an acceptable solution is found, with typically acceptable success rates near 70% or so. The main challenge to deploying this process in our three-dimensional risk preference framework is that we are no longer just dialing up or down the risk of the portfolio and the related width of the Monte Carlo end-horizon outcome set. In our framework, we must moderate three distinct preferences, one of which (loss aversion), is generally moderated toward higher risk portfolios when SLR is high due to the suboptimal nature of highly loss-averse portfolios. An a priori system such as that laid out in Figure 2.8, rather than an iterative, ex-post system to set portfolios and goals such as Monte Carlo simulations, is much more necessary in a more nuanced utility function framework that incorporates both rational and irrational behaviors that moderate in different directions of riskiness. With that said, one can certainly manually modify the portfolio slowly using the three-dimensional map of optimal portfolios reviewed in Chapter 5, and rerun Monte Carlo simulations to finalize a portfolio plan; but the SLR-based moderation system should be a welcome systematic starting place for the process.

As mentioned earlier, one main lever advisors rely on when quoting success rates below 100% is the "flexibility" of the earnings and consumption assumptions baked into the simulation. These goals can indeed be adjusted as time goes on if the client is young enough and open to potential downgrades in future standard of living. I dogmatically avoid this downgrade risk and instead focus on leaving open the opportunity for a standard of living upgrade if the capital markets and savings paths realized are favorable. Of course, as long as the flexibility argument and the potential for failure are clearly presented to the client and well documented, this is certainly a reasonable conversation to have with your client, and one that will certainly require accurate Monte Carlo simulations for proper assessment.

Monte Carlo simulations are a fantastic tool to help understand the variability of future possible wealth outcomes, but I view these as ex post analytics that help verify our ex ante SLR process, or can be used to assess flexibility arguments. In other words, this book recommends starting with what is essentially a straight-line Monte Carlo result (a risk-free investment whose path is totally deterministic) and slowly opening our client portfolios to risk as SLR drops from 100%, with minimal iteration and with near 100% success rate. And when flexibility of goals is on the table, Monte Carlo simulations will bring a relevant layer of information to the advisor's process.

Comparison with Glidepaths

Hopefully, it is now clear that our definition of SLR and how we have translated that into our utility function naturally and explicitly incorporates most of the familiar balance sheet concepts, such as time horizon, goals, human versus financial capital, and so on. But how does this framework compare with the typical glidepath solution?

For those not familiar, a glidepath is a prescribed asset allocation that changes in time assuming you are retiring in X years. There are many different glidepath methods out there, but the best ones I've seen look to maximize income at retirement while minimizing income volatility near retirement (i.e. they maximize ending utility of income) (Moore, Sapra, & Pedersen, 2017). Many of these systems will also account for the volatility of human capital and correlations of human capital with financial assets.

So a typical glidepath solution is similar in the objective it is maximizing to what we are focused on here.[16] However, glidepaths account for human capital as an investable asset while being completely void of any personalized financial goals, whereas, our discretionary wealth framework is squarely focused on achieving a client's personal financial goals without considering the stochastic nature of human capital.

When calculating the tradeoff between a system that includes human capital as an explicit asset but is ignorant of personal cash flow goals, and one that ignores the risk characteristics of human capital yet is cognizant of personal financial goals, I have obviously opted for the latter. This is for three reasons: (1) I believe meeting retirement goals is paramount to any other considerations (as is probably evident from the advocated moderation system focused on a 100% success rate); (2) I want to keep the solutions here simple, confining the discussion to the domain of the single period problem (the glidepath solution is inherently multi-period); and (3) most glidepaths assume bond-like human capital, which is effectively what we are assuming in our discretionary wealth framework. Ideally, we will someday bring the riskiness of human capital into this simplified balance sheet solution, but for now we will stick with our compact SLR approach, due to its simplicity and more stringent focus on achieving a desired standard of living in retirement or multi-generational wealth transfer.

In terms of the difference you can expect between a typical glidepath solution and ours, one must first ask how volatile the human capital is assumed to be in the glidepath approach.[17] On the one hand, very volatile

---

[16]This is an approximation, since the glidepath methodology I have referenced explicitly minimizes income volatility at retirement, whereas our method only implicitly achieves this in a single period format by SLR spiking near retirement conditional on discretionary wealth being low.

[17]In this discussion, I ignore the correlation of human capital with the rest of the portfolio, as well as the labor flexibility of the human capital, consistent with most glidepath approaches. The first omission is motivated by the empirical correlation between human capital and equity investments while the latter omission is based more on omission of these features from most glidepath methods.

human capital (e.g. that of a commodity trader) would require investors to start with very little equity exposure early in their career, which rises in time. On the other hand, low volatility human capital (e.g. that of a tenured professor) would push an investor into higher equity allocations early on, which slowly decrease. As previously noted when justifying our choice of the simpler single-period lifecycle framework, the typical glidepath assumes low volatility human capital, and so we can expect a steadily declining equity allocation from these models into retirement.

Our balance sheet model, on the other hand, is dominated by whether someone is saving properly for retirement. Our most frugal clients will have the lowest SLR (highest equity allocations), as they save aggressively and keep retirement spending goals low. Our least frugal clients will have high SLR's and low equity allocations. For example, a young worker with a reasonable savings plan should be afforded a decent amount of risk early on, given their long stream of expected assets and a liability stream that is so far out that the PV is currently minimal. As liabilities approach closer to one's horizon, discretionary wealth will go down and SLR will rise, and a lower risk portfolio will become more appropriate. Hence, in the case of a "rational" worker with a thoughtful plan for preserving their standard of living in retirement, our client will have an equity allocation in time that looks similar to the typical glidepath. Our framework stands out, though, for people who don't fit nicely in this bucket, where a glidepath solution would certainly let them down due to their less responsible habits. It is the customizable nature of this model that presents the most value.

If you think about it further, our lifecycle model effectively maps the glidepath's human capital riskiness to the risk of being underfunded in retirement (since we have assumed that human capital is bond-like). Most people have steady incomes for employment but are challenged on the saving/spending side of the equation; hence, this swap of focus from human capital riskiness to SLR should be a welcome transition for any wealth management practice.

3

Asset Selection

Step 2 of the four in our journey toward a modern yet practical asset allocation framework answers the following simple question: what assets should I consider for inclusion in a client portfolio? We begin by reviewing a tool that helps identify assets that are accretive to client utility, where we consider utility impacts beyond just the first two moments. We then introduce the second key tool of the chapter that helps ensure our assets have minimal redundancy, a critical requirement to limiting estimation error sensitivity during optimization. By deploying these two methods in the context of risk premia we will be able to quickly establish a well-motivated asset class taxonomy that is simultaneously beneficial to our clients, cognizant of higher moments, and minimal.

Key Takeaways:

1. Systematic asset selection helps ensure that assets are both accretive to utility and generate minimal estimation error sensitivity during optimization, with the knock-on benefit of minimizing the number of asset classes to manage.
2. Cross-asset portfolio moment contributions are a powerful and transparent way of assessing how accretive an asset is to client utility.
3. Mimicking portfolios are deployed to ensure our assets are not redundant, thereby minimizing portfolio sensitivity to estimation error.
4. Application of our two asset selection tools across traditional and alternative risk premia provides for a streamlined taxonomy of asset classes that greatly simplifies the asset selection process.

INTRODUCTION

To date, there has been little focus on rigorous approaches to asset selection within the wealth management industry. The standard approach is to deploy a set of asset classes that has been widely assimilated by the community due to factors such as empirical success of the asset class or popularization by key institutions in the industry. I have a number of issues with this practice. First, this list of popular assets can have as many as 50 categories, a proliferation that adds considerable work to the advisor's load, with unclear additional client benefit. Second, this book goes beyond the second moment in the asset allocation problem, which has not been the typical context for the protagonists above who have established the mainstream asset class list; hence, said list is generally void of higher moment content. And third, any asset allocation framework that is deploying an optimizer (such as the one we are creating here) must be highly selective of portfolio assets to help minimize optimization sensitivity. As reviewed in Chapter 1, a primary cause of optimizer sensitivity is high degrees of comovement between assets; hence, we need to avoid the inclusion of very similar assets in our optimizer. But since most advisors deploying a long list of generally accepted asset classes are not running these assets through an optimizer, the list will not necessarily have been controlled for high degrees of comovement.

There are two main goals of this chapter. First, we want to ensure that all assets input into our optimizer are accretive to a client's utility; and we would like to do so in a manner that is conscious of moment benefits beyond just mean and variance. To this end, we present a model that allows us to see how an asset contributes to moments of a portfolio, giving us a full view into the precise benefit an asset provides to a portfolio, moment-by-moment. Second, we want to be sure to select only those assets with low degrees of comovement (including covariance and higher moment versions such as coskew, cokurtosis, etc.) to help ensure low estimation error sensitivity during optimization. In this vein, we present a model that will help succinctly diagnose redundancy between individual assets, as well as groups of assets, in a single metric that enables swift removal from the portfolio.

When discussing asset selection, there is also the question of completeness: Have we included every possible asset that can improve utility?[1] We could certainly analyze this issue by deploying our newfound moment contribution tool across an exhaustive list of assets and find all those assets showcasing a utility benefit. But this approach is both burdensome and lacks a sense of intuition that would benefit an advisor. Instead, we will pursue a path that combines our two asset selection tools with the world of risk premia. We will explore the most common traditional and alternative risk premia that are investable today, relying on cataloguing that others have

---

[1] One could also ask whether our set of assets covers us across all possible economic scenarios. By virtue of our sample size and stationarity requirements in Chapter 4, which allows us to forecast returns confidently via historical returns, we should be covered for all scenarios.

done for us (Ilmanen, 2011; Hamdan, Pavlowsky, Roncalli, & Zheng, 2016). Applying our two asset selection tools across this catalogue of risk premia will then lead us to a well-motivated asset class taxonomy that is both complete and minimal while accounting for client benefit beyond the first two moments.

As a fun exercise, let's take a big step back from the more mathematical concepts just discussed, and let me propose that a viable asset class should intuitively have the following three broad characteristics:

1. *Client Benefit*: the asset class is beneficial to the client in some way.
2. *Distinct*: there is something unique about the asset class that warrants its inclusion in a portfolio.
3. *Investable*: there is a "straightforward" way to invest in the asset class.[2]

This is exactly what we have already promised to cover: we address client benefit via moment contributions, tackle distinctness via comovement analysis, and ensure assets are investable by only deploying those risk premia currently tracking indices/products. Hopefully, this connection between a more mathematical mandate for asset selection and a very intuitive one compels my readers to trust that the process we are about to outline will ultimately lead us to a very simple and intuitive perspective on asset classes, one that they can confidently deploy in their practice.

Finally, before we jump in, let me be clear that all the calculations we are about to make are based on historical data, with the assumption that this data is a solid forecast for the future behavior of our assets, as this is what we ultimately care about when picking assets. Being able to rely on historical data as forecasts is the topic of Chapter 4, so you will just have to assume for now that the historical data we deploy here is indeed a robust forecast of the future. Ultimately, if Chapter 4 reveals that using history as a forecast is misguided, we would certainly need to double back and rerun our asset selection procedure with our updated forecasts (spoiler alert: in general we will be in good shape but some asset class forecasts will indeed require adjustments to the historical realization).

MOMENT CONTRIBUTIONS

Overview

We begin our asset selection process by addressing the first main goal of the chapter: ensuring assets are accretive to client utility. The key to

---

[2]This includes requirements such as no legal hurdles, low cost, able to absorb investment without moving market, directly investable (no basis risk), etc.

understanding how asset classes improve utility is Eq. (1.4). This equation shows us the relationship between utility and portfolio moments, where each moment provides distinct information about the shape of the portfolio return distribution. That is, the first moment locates the center of the distribution, the second moment describes the width of the distribution, the third and fourth moments characterize how asymmetric and fat-tailed the distribution is respectively, and so on. If we can understand how adding an asset to a portfolio affects the portfolio moments, then we would have a surgical understanding of if and how such an asset is accretive to utility.

Imagine an empty portfolio that we introduce a single asset into. If that asset is normally distributed, then the return of the asset is the sole accretive characteristic to portfolio utility while the volatility is the sole detractor from portfolio utility. But there is an ingredient missing—we currently only have a single asset in the portfolio. What happens when we add another asset? The individual assets' moments are still very important, but now we must also worry about how the return distributions of the two assets diversify each other. In other words, we need to remember the terms such as covariance, coskewness, and cokurtosis, that are embedded in the portfolio moments in Eq. (1.4). Thus, in general, an asset is accretive to a portfolio if it increases utility by adding (subtracting) to beneficial (detrimental) moments on its own or by diversification.

In mean-variance land, we are well versed in this framework: we want to add assets with high returns and low volatility and/or assets that help lower portfolio volatility by being good diversifiers. Here, we are just expanding this concept to all moments, with an added complication that the precise amount of utility that a specific portfolio moment contributes to a portfolio's utility depends on the specific utility function assumed.

Before we describe the mathematical toolkit for moment contributions, let's arm you with some nomenclature on the subject. Assets that increase utility by providing high returns at the expense of a higher moment that is detrimental to the portfolio (e.g. + volatility, − skew, + kurtosis, etc. for power or kinked utility) are known as "performance assets." For example, equities are the preeminent performance asset, providing a substantial expected return relative to bonds at the expense of introducing a moderate yet generally acceptable amount of portfolio volatility. As another example, real estate investing generally raises expected return relative to a diversified bond portfolio at the expense of some unwanted higher moments. However, assets that help raise utility via a higher moment (e.g. − volatility, + skew, − kurtosis, etc. for power or kinked utility) at the cost of lower returns are known as "diversifying assets." For example, bonds are the classic diversifying asset in an equity-centric portfolio, raising utility by lowering portfolio volatility at the expense of an expected return lower than equities. Commodities are another great example of a diversifying asset in a portfolio dominated by equity risk as they generally return less than a diversified equity basket yet they can usually still raise portfolio utility by reducing portfolio volatility.

Hopefully, it is clear at this point that the concept of performance versus diversifying assets is a completely relative concept. You can't label something as a performance or diversifying asset once and forever, since it all depends on the portfolio you are adding the asset to. With that said, people will often label something as a performance asset or diversifying asset without mention of their reference point. But, in these instances, hopefully context clues will assist us.

In the context of diversified multi-asset class investing, one is most likely referencing a traditional diversified portfolio like a 60/40 equity/bond mix. In the context of manager selection or factor investing, one is generally referencing the broad, passive benchmark for the given asset class (e.g. equity value strategies would reference a diversified equity index). For the rest of the book and within my software, we will always be very explicit about what the reference asset is when discussing moment contributions. Additionally, to avoid overcomplicating this analysis, we will generally study moment contributions relative to a single asset class at a time, rather than to a portfolio of assets. The information in this one-to-one comparison is generally enough to inform all necessary asset selection decisions, and it steers us clear of the more convoluted portfolio comparison.

One last subtlety here is that the concept of performance versus diversifying assets is a function of the precise utility being used. In our examples thus far we have assumed our utility function is always increasing and concave, which as discussed in Chapter 1, informs us that high odd moments are detrimental (volatility, kurtosis, etc.), and high even moments are accretive (return, skew, etc.). While this assumption won't hold for every utility function we may deploy, it will still be useful to us, as we are ultimately concerned with building out a generic menu of asset classes with distinct benefits that will serve as the building blocks of our portfolios. Therefore, you should feel free to focus on binning assets as "performance" or "diversifying," assuming preference for odd moments and preference against even moments, even if some of your clients don't have these precise moment preferences; as these assets are just building blocks, the optimizer will ultimately bring to bear the specific utility being addressed. For the remainder of this book, we will assume high odd moment preferences and low even moment preferences when defining performance and diversifying assets.

Calculation

Let's say we want to know how long-term (LT) Treasuries can benefit a portfolio focused on US equities. We are starting with a portfolio that is 100%

invested in US equities, which I will call Asset A, and we want to know how the portfolio's moments would change if we added some LT Treasuries, which will be labeled Asset B. Let's add asset B to the portfolio in a 10% chunk, leaving us with a new portfolio that is 90% allocated to US equities and 10% allocated to LT Treasuries. We can then see how much each portfolio moment changed by adding the 10% slug of asset B, by calculating the change in portfolio moments as

Equation 3.1 Definition of Moment Contributions

$$Moment\ Contribution^i_B = Portfolio\ Moment^i_{90\%\,A+10\%\,B}$$
$$- Portfolio\ Moment^i_{100\%\,A}$$

where i is the moment number and goes from 1 to infinity (but we are only focused on the first four moments), B is the asset being analyzed, and A is the asset we are judging asset B against. Note that all statistics presented are calculated from monthly time series and not modified away from their monthly form (i.e. they are not annualized).

This is actually a very important topic we need to pause on. Everything presented in this book will be calculated and presented in monthly terms. The reason for this is twofold: (1) private clients indeed care if their portfolio grossly underperforms over a one month period hence we should calculate utility and all relevant statistics on a monthly horizon; and (2) while it is generally straightforward to scale monthly returns and volatility to longer horizons, the same cannot be said of higher moments (Neuberger & Payne, 2018); hence, we always present the monthly estimates.

Figure 3.1 reviews the moment contribution calculation defined by Eq. (3.1) for our LT Treasury/US equities example (ignoring the last column for now, which we introduce in the next section). The first line shows the portfolio moments before the Treasuries are added, the second line shows the new portfolio moments when a 10% slug of Treasuries is introduced, and the last row shows the final moment contribution results. We see that introducing LT Treasuries to a portfolio of US equities, with the specific indices and forecasted distributions considered,[3] reduces portfolio volatility (highlighted by the box) without introducing any large negative effects in

---

[3]In this example we use monthly returns from 1972 to 2018, where LT Treasuries are represented by a constant maturity 30-year index provided by the Center for Research in Security Prices at the University of Chicago's Booth School of Business (CRSP®) and US equities are represented by the value-weight return of all CRSP firms incorporated in the US and listed on the NYSE, AMEX, or NASDAQ that

	Monthly Return	Monthly Volatility	Monthly Skew	Monthly Kurtosis	Monthly Utility
100% US Equities	0.92%	4.47%	−0.54	5.15	0.846
90% US Equities & 10% LT Treasuries	0.89%	4.05%	−0.47	4.93	0.874
Contribution of LT Treasuries	−0.03%	−0.42%	0.07	−0.22	3.3%

FIGURE 3.1 Moment Contribution Example: Long-Term Treasuries Added to a US Equity Portfolio (Utility Parameters: $\gamma = 6$, $\lambda = 3$, $\varphi = 0$)

other moments. Since the asset is predominantly driving down volatility, it is clearly a diversifying asset in this context. This example highlights the classic logic behind investing in a mix of bonds and equities within the mean-variance framework: volatility can be greatly reduced while not overly burdening the portfolio's expected return.

In the above example we analyzed the value of one broad asset against another broad (yet distinct) asset. One can just as easily run this analysis against a closer cousin, for example, an equity value strategy versus equities. Additionally, one could deploy this tool as a manager selection device, where asset A represents a particular fund being researched as an actively managed solution to be slotted in for asset B.

Harkening back to our performance versus diversifying assets categorization, one can now certainly take that taxonomy one step further by delineating the exact moment that dominates the asset's utility contribution. In the example above we can now say that bonds are a diversifying asset by way of lowering volatility. As another example, many performance assets predominantly contribute negative skew rather than positive volatility—a truism in the case of deep equity value strategies, if we are considering adding the strategy to a portfolio of equities. In this case we would classify deep value as a negative skew performance asset.

Some of you may be getting the feeling that this concept of moment contributions is a strange form of factor model where in some fashion we have substituted risk factors with moments. A moment contribution analysis directly connects to the purpose of the asset, which is to provide benefit to

---

have a CRSP share code of 10 or 11, sourced from Ken French's online library. In Chapter 4, we will justify the use of historical data for our forecasts of these two assets.

client utility, while a factor model identifies the underlying drivers of returns for a more complete understanding of the asset, but with no connection to the portfolio's value for a client. A risk factor model is a welcome risk management tool in any asset allocator's toolkit to ensure there are no unknown bets being made in a portfolio, but it fundamentally doesn't address whether an asset is accretive to the client portfolio. In this book our main concern with risk factors is that the assets we select for inclusion in client portfolios should cover us in all substantial (i.e. higher likelihood) risk factor regimes, but by virtue of our sample and stationarity assumptions outlined in Chapter 4 we will assume we are covered here.

Utility Contribution

Up to this point we have still not explicitly accounted for our client's utility function in our asset selection process. The framework thus far has been focused on moment contributions, completely ignorant of how sensitive our client is to each moment until we account for the exact utility function parameters. For instance, a client with loss aversion $\lambda = 3$ will be more sensitive to skew contributions than a client with $\lambda = 1$. In addition, we have been silent on the topic when it comes to cases where $\varphi = 1$ and our utility is reflective, since we have assumed preference solely for higher odd moments, which is only guaranteed in the case of power or kinked utilities ($\varphi = 0$). To account for both issues, we now introduce a utility contribution tool, that accounts for the precise utility function preferences of our client.

Utility contribution is very similar to moment contribution defined in Eq. (3.1), except now we assess changes in portfolio utility rather than individual moments. As laid out in Eq. (3.2), to find the utility contribution from asset B, we calculate the change in total utility from a portfolio with a single asset A to a portfolio that replaces 10% of asset A with a chunk of asset B.

Equation 3.2 Formal Definition of Utility Contribution

$$Utility\ Contribution_B = (Portfolio\ Utility_{90\%\ A+10\%\ B} - Portfolio\ Utility_{100\%\ A})$$
$$/Portfolio\ Utility_{100\%\ A}$$

In contrast to our moment contribution formula earlier, we are now also normalizing the calculation by the starting portfolio utility since the units of utility are meaningless. For instance, it is very transparent what a first moment contribution of 0.5% means: the portfolio expected monthly return is going up a half a percent by adding 10% of the asset being considered.

However, saying an asset raises utility by five means nothing to us, since utility is ordinal. Hence the easiest way to assign benefit of an asset from a utility standpoint is to measure the percentage change in utility when we add the new asset to the portfolio. The last column of Figure 3.1 extends our earlier example of adding LT Treasuries to a US equity portfolio to account for utility contribution. As you can see, for a client with strong risk and loss aversion but no reflection ($\gamma = 6, \lambda = 3, \varphi = 0$), the volatility benefit provided by just a 10% slug in Treasuries indeed helps improve the client's portfolio utility by 3.3%.

Let's pause at this point and note that the moment contribution framework presented earlier is in many ways completely sufficient for our purpose of asset selection. That tool allowed us to assess which assets provided distinguished contributions by moment, which can fully enable us to create an asset menu for our optimizer with varied distribution types that fully span all possible moment preferences. Whether or not an asset adds utility for a specific three-dimensional client profile is truly in the realm of the optimizer, regarding how much exposure it should give a particular asset with its particular distribution. Hence, this utility contribution tool is of secondary importance for asset selection; it is deployed as more of an interesting window into a detail (accounting for the precise utility function) that the optimizer will have the distinguished pleasure of ultimately managing.

MIMICKING PORTFOLIOS

We are now ready to attack the second main goal of the chapter, which is to avoid deploying assets with high levels of comovement, whether that be covariance, coskew, or any higher order comovement.[4] Additionally, we are not just interested in comovement between individual assets, we are also interested in the comovement of each asset against a synthetic replication of

---

[4] We also don't want to be too blunt or hasty in our pursuit of orthogonality either else we risk losing some potentially interesting utility benefits. For example, the grouping of Treasuries and high-yield bonds would not be redundant with equities, but we have also lost the ability to tune the breakdown between duration and credit if we group these assets together. To this end, one should only group assets that are very similar into a single asset class, a feature known as internal homogeneity. To ensure we haven't lumped our assets into groups that are unnecessarily broad, we should always study comovement among assets that we have even the slightest sense may offer distinctness from their closest cousins, and then slowly group assets into broader categories once we are sure we are not missing any asset-specific benefit.

that asset using other assets, since our optimizer will be very sensitive to this kind of overlap as well.

If you think about it, an asset can't add utility to a portfolio when it is redundant to a single asset or set of assets within the portfolio. Hence, being accretive to utility relative to an existing portfolio subsumes the problem of redundancy. However, deploying our moment or utility contribution techniques at the portfolio level for this purpose would be unnecessarily complicated. Instead, we introduce the concept of a mimicking portfolio (Kinlaw, Kritzman, & Turkington, 2017)—the portfolio of all other assets—which tracks the asset under investigation as closely as possible. If the tracking error between the mimicking portfolio and the asset under consideration is high, then the asset is not redundant. However, if a portfolio of assets can be created that looks very similar to the asset we are considering, then the asset is redundant and should not be selected for inclusion in the portfolio.

More formally, the mimicking portfolio for asset B using the N assets labeled 1, 2, ..., N, is the portfolio defined by weights a_1, a_2, ... a_N that minimizes the sum of squared differences of returns between the synthetic portfolio and asset B:

Equation 3.3 Definition of Mimicking Portfolio

$$\min_{a_1,a_2,\ldots,a_N} \sum_{i=1}^{s} \left(r^i_{mimicking\ portfolio} - r^i_B \right)^2$$

where r^i_B are monthly returns for asset B and $r^i_{mimicking\ portfolio} = a_1 r^i_1 + a_2 r^i_2 + \ldots + a_N r^i_N$ are the monthly returns for the mimicking portfolio, where all coefficients a_1 to a_N are between 0 and 1 and their sum equals 1.

This minimization problem is what is known as a "constrained linear least squares," since we deploy "constraints" on the coefficients of the "linear" superposition of assets in our mimicking portfolio while optimizing for the "least" "squares" of the differences between the mimicking portfolio and asset B. Some of you may be familiar with least squares solvers, as this is the most common technique used to solve a linear regression. The main difference between our solution here and the standard linear regression is that we have constraints (size and sum) on the coefficients of the regression.[5]

---

[5]For those who would like to contemplate shifting this replication to an unconstrained regression model in order to leverage some of the textbook regression results like coefficient *t*-stats, etc., I will warn you that the residuals will not typically be normally distributed, hence the textbook regression toolkit will not apply.

Once we have the mimicking portfolio for an asset, we can judge its redundancy by looking at the tracking error between the mimicking portfolio and the asset. The mimicking portfolio tracking error (MPTE) is defined as

Equation 3.4 Definition of Mimicking Portfolio Tracking Error

$$MPTE = \text{Standard Deviation } (r_{mimicking\ portfolio} - r_B)$$

If the mimicking portfolio closely resembles asset B, then the MPTE will be low, and asset B is redundant and should be avoided to avoid estimation error sensitivity. However, if the MPTE for asset B is high, then the asset clearly showcases distinctness in one or more moments and can potentially be a valuable asset to consider for the portfolio. We emphasize "potentially," since an asset is not necessarily accretive to the client just because it is distinct (but the opposite is true, as discussed earlier in this section). Hence, if an asset has a minuscule MPTE to all relevant assets, it can be avoided with complete confidence.

Figure 3.2 takes the reader through a quick example.[6] We start with a portfolio of three assets, intermediate-term Treasuries, intermediate-term investment grade (IG) bonds, and high-yield bonds (whose duration is close to intermediate term), and find the mimicking portfolio for each asset from the two other assets in the portfolio. The tracking error between the mimicking portfolio and the asset under consideration is shown in the first column.

	MPTE	Monthly Return Contribution	Monthly Volatility Contribution	Monthly Skew Contribution	Monthly Kurtosis Contribution
Intermediate Term Treasuries	0.91%	−0.041%	−0.45%	0.008	0.01
Intermediate Term IG Bonds	0.51%	−0.037%	−0.40%	−0.012	0.11
High Yield Bonds	1.72%	−0.031%	−0.30%	−0.043	0.26

FIGURE 3.2 MPTE Example: Fixed Income

---

[6]In this example we use monthly returns from 1/1994 to 2/2019 from VFITX, VFICX, and VWEHX, publicly available proxies for intermediate-term Treasuries, intermediate-term IG bonds, and high-yield bonds respectively. VFICX inception of 11/1993 prevented us from going back further in time for the analysis.

As you can see, no MPTE exceeds 2%, which is a reasonable level below which to start flagging assets for potential removal due to redundancy. For reference, if one were to compare a set of broad asset classes such as equities versus bonds versus commodities, we would expect monthly MPTE in the range of 3–5%, where we have zero expectation of redundancy.

It is interesting to note that, of the three assets presented in Figure 3.2, it is IG bonds which are flagging as most redundant. Intuitively this makes sense, since this asset has roughly equal amounts of duration exposure and credit exposure, which is precisely a superposition of duration-dominated Treasuries and credit-dominated high-yield bonds. And this is precisely the message we get from the moment contributions (vs. US equities), also shown in Figure 3.2. We see that the safer Treasuries are the strongest volatility-improving asset relative to equities with their pure duration focus; while at the other end of the spectrum, high-yield bonds look more like a performance asset, at the expense of increased negative skew and less volatility improvement relative to equities; while the IG bond asset lies smack in the middle of these two assets in terms of moment contributions relative to equities.

We just started to deploy the framework of risk premia (duration, credit, etc.) to help us understand moment contributions and redundancy. Let's now fully leverage the concept of risk premia in conjunction with our moment contribution and MPTE models to create a systematic taxonomy of asset classes that is both complete and minimal.

A NEW ASSET CLASS PARADIGM

Overview

Thus far we have provided tools that help us assess on a case-by-case basis whether an asset is both accretive to utility and lacking overlap with other assets in the portfolio. This one-off use of the tools can be time-consuming; hence, we would ideally have a means of streamlining the asset selection process from this highly bespoke system. But we just saw in the case of bonds that, by understanding the underlying risk premia at play, one could a priori build intuition behind both redundancy and moment contributions. In this manner, risk premia are a convenient means to help simplify the full cataloguing of assets one would like to consider.

Additionally, risk premia by definition should offer relatively stable reward for the risk you are bearing over long time horizons (10+ years). By grouping assets by their risk premium, we are also adding in a layer of confidence as to the future reliability of the return source (stay tuned for more rigorous testing of return reliability in Chapter 4). In the remainder of the chapter we will thus leverage the full taxonomy of risk premia, in conjunction with our two asset selection tools, to build an intuitive menu of asset classes that is complete, beneficial to clients, and minimal. And as you will see, this exercise will also help demonstrate why higher order moments are increasingly important with the evolution of smart beta products.

A Review of Risk Premia

To create a complete yet succinct view of risk premia it is convenient to note that they can be divided into four camps: traditional risk premia; geographic risk premia; skewness risk premia; and market anomalies. The last two together comprise what is known as alternative risk premia, AKA style premia, factor investing, or smart beta.

Traditional risk premia (TRP) compensate an investor for holding a passive, long-only basket of a specific security type. The preeminent traditional risk premia we will focus on are equity, duration, real estate, and commodities (Ilmanen, 2012). Traditional risk premia are all beneficial relative to a risk-free asset as performance assets. But within a diversified portfolio, the equity and real estate premia are predominantly beneficial to a portfolio by providing high first moments (performance assets) while the duration and commodity premia predominantly help lower the second moment (diversifying assets).

Absent from our above list of four TRP are several security types such as credit, currencies, private equity, art, and a few other categories one may consider to be a distinct traditional asset class. Any security type missing from the four mentioned above is missing for one of three reasons: (1) the asset class doesn't offer a robust TRP, and we generally steer clear of assets that don't produce some form of long-term expected return (e.g. currencies); (2) the asset class doesn't offer distinct value to client utility (e.g. credit[7]); and (3) the asset class is illiquid, and according to our assumptions throughout this book we are only including liquid investment categories (e.g. private equity).

Then there is the geographic risk premium (GRP). Most of us are probably aware that we can potentially earn a higher first moment if we are willing to accept the additional risk associated with investing in riskier countries or regions. For example, US equities are generally expected to earn less than emerging market equities due to this reality (Donadelli & Prosperi, 2011).

---

[7]One can most easily see this by looking at the small MPTE of credit when grouped with the other four TRP, or by noticing that, while credit helps reduce volatility relative to equities (but to a lesser extent than duration), it does not add much return relative to duration and hence it is not a distinctly useful asset.

In theory, this same logic should apply to emerging market sovereign debt (duration) and real estate, but not commodities, since these are not tied to a region or country. The geographic risk premium is then an added layer of premium that we must account for in all asset classes besides commodities. To decide which GRP are important to invest in within the three TRP where a GRP is relevant, we must assess the moment contributions and MPTE of different geographies. And from what I can tell, this premium is only compelling and distinct when comparing developed versus emerging markets, with the value being a lot lower and redundant when comparing US versus other developed markets. Hence, I will steer clear of the common practice of breaking geographies into three categories (US, developed foreign, and emerging) and limit our discussion to just US versus emerging. I certainly could've tried to avoid "home bias" by opting for developed (US + foreign) rather than just US, but from an investment product coverage standpoint I think it is a bit easier to stick with the US as our developed market proxy (it also currently dominates the developed global market cap anyway).

Alternative risk premia (ARP) are distinct premia harvested by layering an active strategy on top of a TRP + GRP combination. ARP can be broken up into two categories: skewness risk premia and market anomalies (Roncalli, 2017). On the one hand, skewness risk premia include those strategies that compensate an investor for accepting additional negative skew relative to the underlying universe.. Market anomalies, on the other hand, are those strategies overlaid on TRP + GRP that provide compensation to an investor without additional risk-taking in the form of additional negative skew relative to the underlying universe. Hopefully it is now clear why we separate these two types of strategy: one entails introducing additional risk into the portfolio while the other does not. Let's now review the canonical forms of these two types of strategies to help us build a powerful framework for understanding ARP in general.

The reversal strategy is the simplest and most explicit template for a skewness risk premium one can imagine. We start with an equity index, and increasingly go long (short) the index as it drops below (rises above) a target price, with the expectation that we will profit when the price reverts to the mean. It can be shown that this strategy (with some simple Brownian motion assumptions baked into it) will have a positive Sharpe ratio and a positive premium relative to the underlying at the expense of introducing negative skew relative to the starting universe. One can also show that this strategy's skew is in sync with drawdowns in the underlying universe; hence, it is a concave strategy, which means it behaves like you are shorting a straddle, where you outperform during typical market environments and then underperform during extreme negative or extreme positive market environments.

Figure 3.3 presents a visual representation of a concave strategy by plotting asset returns versus the underlying TRP's returns. We see the TRP

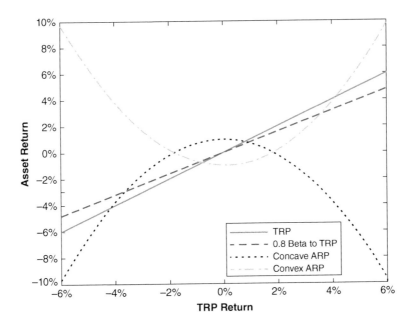

FIGURE 3.3 Payoffs of Concave and Convex ARP

asset itself track a 45-degree line when plotted against the TRP returns, as expected. We also show an asset which is linearly related to the TRP via a coefficient (beta) of 0.8, which provides a graphical representation of what a linear relation between two assets looks like. We then show the payoff of a concave ARP like the reversal strategy, where we see the strategy outperform in calm to slightly down markets. It underperforms in more extreme markets, though admittedly more so in strong up periods, which jives with our intuition behind the strategy's concavity.

It is critical to pause and process just how non-linear the relative payoff is for this ARP, which is one of the key reasons why we have pushed so hard toward a full utility optimization that accounts for more than just covariance (which only accounts for purely linear relationships between assets). Soon we will go beyond the textbook reversal strategy when it comes to skewness risk premia, which will include strategies with varying degrees of non-linearity; but hopefully at this point we have convinced the reader that the mention of ARP should always raise antennas as to their degree of non-linearity.

The textbook template for a market anomaly is the trend-following strategy. Starting again with an equity index, this strategy increasingly goes long (short) the index as momentum is increasingly positive (negative), with the expectation that recent performance trends will continue. This strategy will also have a positive Sharpe ratio—but now with positive skew and a convex payoff relative to the underlying index, creating the relative performance of a long straddle (where the strategy underperforms during average markets but outperforms during extreme negative or extreme positive markets). Unlike the reversal strategy, the trend-following strategy will not necessarily have a positive premium relative to the underlying. A true market anomaly, though, will have convex characteristics alongside a positive premium relative to the underlying (hence why we call it an "anomaly").

Again, the convex payoff for market anomalies is illustrated in Figure 3.3, where we see the strategy shine during large drawdowns of the TRP but consistently underperform during average markets. Hopefully, it is now clear that beyond ARP raising antennas on payoff linearity, one should ask whether the ARP is more of a coupon-clipping skewness risk premia that will consistently perform well except under extreme conditions (a form of selling insurance), or a market anomaly strategy that consistently underperforms but with the benefit of some large timely wins in extreme markets (a form of buying insurance). One should expect that as one adds concavity to an ARP the premium over the underlying should go up while as one adds convexity to an ARP the premium should go down, as we create increasingly performance and diversifying assets, respectively.

Alternative risk premia are rampant across security types (equities, bonds, currencies, etc.); hence, one should consider these potentially higher moment focused investment strategies not just in equities, as reviewed thus far, but across instrument types. Figure 3.4 summarizes whether an alternative risk premium exists in a given asset class. There are hundreds of ARP identified to date, but in the figure I am just focusing on the TRP we are

	Equities	Duration	Real Estate	Commodities
Carry	✓	✓	✓	✓
Momentum	✓	✓	✓	✓
Value	✓	✓	✓	✓
Volatility	✓	✓	✓	✓
Low Volatility	✓		✓	
Quality	✓		✓	

FIGURE 3.4 Preeminent Traditional and Alternative Risk Premia

concerned with and the preeminent ARP (i.e. largest and best documented positive premia relative to their underlying) that are also tied to investment products today.[8]

In Figure 3.4 we see that carry, momentum, value, and volatility risk premia and anomalies are pervasive amongst all TRP we focus on. There are also two style premia we focus on that only exist within equities and real estate: low volatility and quality. Let's quickly review the definition of each ARP for completeness.

"Carry" strategies capture a rate spread—a famous example being overweight higher yielding equities, but is easily extended to yield curves, currencies, and so on. "Momentum" overweights the strongest performing assets and comes in both a cross-sectional variety, AKA relative momentum, where you overweight the top relative performers in a group (the classic Fama-French variety), as well as a trend-following variety, AKA absolute momentum or time-series momentum, where you invest in positive performers and short or avoid negative performers (an example of which is the textbook convex strategy just reviewed). "Value" bets on undervalued securities to mean revert (mechanically very similar to the reversal strategy discussed earlier). They can be configured to work on both ultra-short (1 month) and intermediate (3–5 year) horizons, a nice ballast to the short (6–12 month) horizon that momentum works on. "Volatility" bets on implied volatility being inflated relative to future realized volatility. It is a form of insurance selling also known as "shorting volatility," since you are selling implied volatility. "Low volatility" bets on those entities with the lowest historical volatilities, contrary to beliefs popularized by the CAPM that higher volatility (higher beta) entities should outperform. Finally, "quality" invests in those securities with the highest quality balance sheets, which, similar to low volatility, is somewhat counterintuitive.

Now, which of these would you assume offers a skewness risk premium and which would you think would fall under the anomaly camp? If you try to answer this from a fundamental perspective, you will struggle, because you are asking the surprisingly challenging question of whether you are being compensated for taking on a clearly defined risk. There is an incredible amount of literature on justifying risk premia from a risk-taking

---

[8]This graphic is a consolidated version of a graphic derived in a wonderful manuscript that reviewed style premia actually connected to investable indices or products (Hamdan, Pavlowsky, Roncalli, & Zheng, 2016). I have taken the liberty of curating a short list of ARP that are most compelling and most pervasive in practice.

perspective, and there are still many open questions in this arena.[9] It is much simpler to ask whether a style premium will protect you when its respective TRP struggles. If it does, then you are dealing with a market anomaly, and if it doesn't, you are dealing with a skewness risk premium. It is then rather intuitive to bin momentum, low volatility, and quality as the only anomalies on the list, as they can help preserve capital when the associated traditional risk premium struggles. The remaining ARP highlighted in Figure 3.3, including carry, value, and volatility, are then all skewness risk premia.

One thing that is critical to note about ARP is that, unlike TRP and GRP, there are an incredible number of variations possible for each ARP. There is no standard way necessarily to access these premia, making it very difficult to easily access the textbook (and admittedly maximally caricatured) distribution properties presented earlier. Let's consider momentum. We already mentioned there were two types: cross-sectional and trend-following. In addition, the strategy will generally be created in either a long-only format or a long/short format, where the former will provide exposure to the underlying TRP + GRP and the latter will not. Next, the precise parameters used to fully define the strategy (e.g. how momentum is measured, when positions are sold, etc.) can have a big impact on the final return distribution characteristics. Then there is the concentration of the portfolio, which also magnifies or dims the effect of the ARP relative to the TRP. And there is a big distinction within momentum strategies between using constituents with less or more correlation, with the former generally creating more positive skew. I could continue, but hopefully this demonstrates that just because someone labels a strategy as "momentum" does not guarantee specific monthly return distribution characteristics. There are indeed many momentum strategies that do not offer positive premia, positive skew, or positive convexity.[10] As ARP become more mainstream, and higher moments are increasingly focused on, I am sure the asset management industry will increasingly focus on a more surgical creation of precise ARP distributions, along with more precise use cases for clients.

---

[9]With that said, an intuitive perspective on this topic that seems to work nicely is analyzing the problem via the mechanics of the strategy. If the strategy is adding to "losers," then you are providing liquidity in assets that the market perceives as a bad investment and are being paid a premium to take on that risk. If the strategy is adding to "winners," though, one is in the opposite situation and cannot be receiving compensation for a risk being expressed by market participants.

[10]One reference I like on the empirical performance of different ARP is by Lemperiere, et al. (Lemperiere, et al., 2014).

From Assets to Asset Classes

We are now ready to take our newfound understanding of risk premia and, by combining this with our asset selection process laid out earlier, define a succinct set of asset classes to deploy in client portfolios. Figure 3.5 summarizes a workflow that allows you to go quickly from an extensive list of assets to a short set of well-motivated asset classes that will play nicely with an optimizer.

We begin the asset class definition process by assessing the moment contributions and MPTE of the key traditional risk premia against each other, which should be focused heavily on the first and second moments of each TRP relative to one another. We then assess moment contributions and MPTE for different geographies within each traditional category to see if there is a valuable geographic risk premium to be had. Finally, we pit style premia against their underlying asset class benchmark (accounting for geography) to investigate their value-add relative to a passive deployment of the traditional premium. At this level we are more focused on higher moments than we were during the first two steps of the process, given ARP tendencies to tilt higher moments.

Figure 3.6 presents my take on a reasonable set of asset classes based on the system just laid out, considering not just moment contributions and

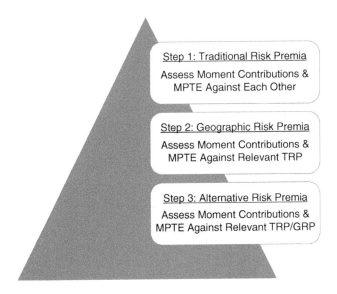

FIGURE 3.5 Workflow for Creating an Asset Class Menu

Performance Assets	Diversifying Assets
Equities - Domestic - Div. LO ARP	Duration - Domestic - Passive
Equities - Emerging - Passive	Duration - Emerging - Passive
Real Estate - Domestic - Passive	Commodities - Passive
	Equities - Domestic - Div. l/s ARP

FIGURE 3.6   A New Asset Class Taxonomy

redundancy, but also what is easily accessible within the wealth management space today, as well as tractability for implementation. We start with coverage at the top level from all four TRP bearing a clear and distinct risk premium. We then include emerging versus US coverage within the two TRP where it is most accessible (equities and sovereign debt, not real estate). We finish with a diversified long-only ARP overlay within domestic equities, as well as a stand-alone diversified long/short (l/s) ARP asset class built off domestic equities (we will justify this shortly).[11]

In the previous section we already justified consolidation to just four TRPs and 2 GRPs, so let's now dig into the ARP decisions. The top half of Figure 3.7 shows the moment contribution analysis (relative to US equities) applied to a couple of Fama-French (F-F) long-only (LO) ARP. The high minus low (HML) factor is our proxy for a core skewness risk premium, of the value type, and the robust minus weak (RMW) factor is our proxy for a core market anomaly, of the quality type. We see typical performance asset benefits from HML (+ return, + volatility, − skew) and slight diversifying asset benefits with positive excess return from RMW (+ return, − volatility), roughly in line with our expectations for skewness risk premia and market anomalies, respectively.[12] In this analysis, we also show how a balanced portfolio of the two ARP (which, from here on, we will use as our US equity diversified LO ARP asset) benefits an equity portfolio.

---

[11]We don't split the convex and concave ARPs into two distinct asset classes within long-only domestic equities or l/s domestic equities because the ARP we are using provide positive premia relative to the underlying and as such are not distinct enough re: distribution shape to warrant such an organization. To go down that road one would need to deploy extremely convex assets with negative expected excess premia.
[12]In this example, we use monthly returns from 1972 to 2018, where US equities (contribution benchmark) are represented by the value-weight return of all CRSP firms incorporated in the US and listed on the NYSE, AMEX, or NASDAQ that have a CRSP share code of 10 or 11, and HML and RMW follow standard definitions, all sourced from Ken French's online library.

	Monthly Return	Monthly Volatility	Monthly Skew	Monthly Kurtosis
F-F HML Top Quintile	0.03%	0.01%	−0.01	−0.02
F-F RMW Top Quintile	0.01%	−0.02%	0.00	0.05
1/2 F-F HML Top Quintile + 1/2 F-F RMW Top Quintile	0.02%	0.00%	−0.01	0.01
F-F HML	−0.06%	−0.52%	−0.02	0.10
F-F RMW	−0.06%	−0.50%	0.02	0.04
1/2 F-F HML + 1/2 F-F RMW	−0.06%	−0.51%	0.00	0.07

FIGURE 3.7 ARP Moment Contributions

This diversified long-only ARP exposure within domestic equities ultimately leans toward being a performance asset, as it generally adds a couple percent per year of performance as a standalone investment (remember, Figure 3.7 quotes monthly contributions of a 10% slug). The cost is lowering skew and adding kurtosis to the portfolio, relative to a core US equity holding. And to be clear, we do not separate this LO ARP investment into a distinct asset class from passive US equities in Figure 3.6, because there would be too much comovement between the two asset classes.

The second half of Figure 3.7 reviews the l/s version of the analysis we just completed, where we now see that the equal combination of the same two factors in l/s format, in line with the formal Fama-French definitions of the factors, leads to a clear diversifying asset relative to US equities. This asset has similar characteristics relative to equities as duration (−return, −volatility) but with even better volatility reduction characteristics. Here, the cost is worsened skew and kurtosis (30-year Treasuries have −0.42% volatility contribution, 0.07 skew contribution, and −0.22 kurtosis contribution), as one may expect from the asset's ARP nature relative to duration.[13]

---

[13]It is fun to compare the results of Figure 3.7 to those in Figure 1.3. In Figure 3.7, we see contributions to skew and kurtosis relative to equities that are potentially much different than many may expect from the stand-alone asset skew and kurtosis

The fact that this l/s asset diversifies duration (statistics not shown here), and can actually improve volatility of an equity-dominated portfolio better than duration, explains why we include this asset as an asset class.

This asset class can be viewed as a liquid alternative investment, acting similar to the core proposition of less liquid l/s hedge funds, where they can diversify equity beta even better than duration. This is a key feature that will stand out in Chapter 5, when we review our optimized portfolios as a function of our three-dimensional client preference space. From here on, we will deploy this equal combination of F-F HML and RMW factors as our US equity diversified l/s ARP asset.

It is comforting to see our asset class taxonomy have some familiar features with today's popular asset class systems: we see a broad distribution of security types and geographies, alongside diversified exposure to style premia. But there are probably more differences than similarities between this asset class list and those most commonly used today. The most glaring distinction is that there is just one level of asset classes, not a tiered hierarchy. This advantage precludes the need to do optimizations in two stages (i.e. first *within* equities, fixed income, real estate, etc., and then on the combination of those optimized sub-portfolios). This set of seven asset classes is also very small compared to the typical 15–30 commonly deployed. This short length stems from our strict mandate to include only assets with clear utility benefit and high MPTE, with the additional mandate of having substantial and stable risk premia, avoiding unnecessary proliferation of assets for the sake of looking busy or smart.

I think the set of asset classes presented is complete, minimal, and relevant to the client utility maximization problem we are looking to solve. With that said, there are certainly other possible outcomes of the asset selection process just outlined. The final set of asset classes just presented is certainly biased by what I personally judge to be a worthwhile level of moment contribution for including coverage, an MPTE I find sufficiently low for avoidance, and an availability in the marketplace I deem sufficient. For instance, one could have looked to a multi-asset class diversified l/s ARP to include in the portfolio (rather than an equity-based one), or pivoted from a US-focused developed equity exposure to a global version. With that said, as long as the value-add of the asset class is clear and an optimizer can successfully handle your taxonomy, then you should be in good shape. The goal of the chapter

---

results in Figure 1.3. For example, in Figure 3.7 the F-F HML skew contribution is negative despite a stand-alone asset skew in Figure 1.3 that is much higher than US equities, due to the fact that HML is a skewness risk premium. As such, it has a concave payoff relative to the underlying TRP, which reduces portfolio skew (via coskew) at a faster pace than its small stand-alone skew can increase portfolio skew.

was to introduce the reader to a new set of tools and a new perspective on a topic so often overlooked, and ultimately provide just one reasonable solution to the problem at hand.

Some readers may be wondering where the myriad other assets not encompassed by our seven asset classes are; for example, in the fixed income space we haven't talked about mortgage-backed securities. These other assets in general provide limited extra benefit in the way of moment contributions or are too redundant with the core TRP asset class already included. With that said, there are indeed times when these niche markets will provide attractive buying opportunities relative to our core asset class. So we certainly want to keep track of those markets and deploy them within their relevant asset class as opportunities arise, if the advisor is so inclined. Inclusion of these assets presenting short- to intermediate-term trading opportunities can indeed be accounted for in our framework by altering the forecast for the core asset class, a key topic within the broader discussion we will now have in Chapter 4, on capital market assumptions.

4

Capital Market Assumptions

In this chapter we continue down the path of returns-based expected utility optimization. We will create the joint return distribution forecast to feed into our optimizer, alongside the client utility function. Our starting point for this process is the full set of historical monthly returns for the assets we have selected. We introduce two techniques that help diagnose whether the historical return series is a reliable source for future expectations. The chapter ends with a review of how to modify our historical monthly return dataset for custom forecasts, manager selection, fees, and taxes.

Key Takeaways:

1. In a returns-based asset allocation framework we require a forecast for the full distribution of future joint returns as input to our optimizer.
2. We deploy historical return distributions as our baseline forecast, given the simplicity and zero approximation error introduced into the estimation process.
3. Bootstrapped standard errors are introduced to measure whether historical returns are providing sufficient estimation accuracy.
4. Historical return distributions are only useful forecasts if they are stationary—that is, their properties are stable over long periods, a feature we test with the Kolmogorov–Smirnov test.
5. We adjust historical distributions to account for custom market views, manager alpha, and fees via a simple shift of the return distributions.
6. Taxes are accounted for via a more nuanced combination of shifting and scaling of the historical return distributions.

INTRODUCTION

Thus far, we have fully specified our client's utility function by careful assessment of their risk preferences and financial situation. And we have chosen the assets that are worthwhile for us to include in our client's portfolio.

The last thing we must do before running our optimizer is create the full set of possible outcomes as required by Eq. (1.2), where each outcome is a joint monthly return for all of our assets. We are not forecasting individual moments or co-moments, as is done in mean-variance asset allocation; rather, we are forecasting every single possible combination of monthly returns our assets could ever experience. Since this is an incredibly challenging task (given the complexity of financial markets which lead to joint return distributions of nuanced shape), we must look for a simple way to do this. Luckily, we can use the historical joint return distribution for our assets as our baseline forecast.

As discussed in Chapter 1, there are two conditions that must be met for a historical monthly return distribution to be a good forecast over long horizons. The first is that our sample size T (the number of monthly data points we have) must be large to ensure the accuracy of our estimation, as you need many data points to accurately diagnose the properties of a distribution. To this end, we introduce the concept of standard error, which we use to measure the uncertainty of the moment estimates that are embedded in the historical distributions we are deploying (we say "embedded" because we don't actually deploy the moment estimate in our model; we just analyze the moment error bars as a validation tool). Second, our return distribution must be stationary over long horizons so that we can assume the past will represent the future. To this end, we introduce the Kolmogorov–Smirnov test, which informs us whether the return distribution from one long period resembles the return distribution from a previous long period, indicating a stable return process where history can be trusted as a forecast.

We will also need to be able to modify the forecasts encapsulated by the historical distribution. There are many reasons why one would want to modify the historical distribution before inputting it into the optimizer. One may want to account for secular trends in risk premia. Many advisors also want to pursue active managers who can add alpha to the core asset class proposition. Fees and taxes are also critical components of real-world investments that should be accounted for. To this end, we will introduce a simple system for adjusting historical return distributions for these typical situations by shifting the entire monthly return distribution by a constant (except for capital gains taxes, which require a scaling of returns due to the government's active partnership in sharing our losses).

But before we get into the weeds, the reader might be wondering why the litany of popularized forecasting models are in a chapter on capital market assumptions (for a nice review of many of these, see Maginn, Tuttle, Pinto, & McLeavey, 2007). First, there is the question of timeframe. From the very beginning we have been focused on 10-year forecasts and beyond, precluding the use of any models with a tactical forecasting horizon

(6–12 months) or opportunistic forecasting horizon (3–5 years). This removes from our purview both price-based momentum and mean reversion models, along with most fundamental models (e.g. the dividend discount model where dividend and growth forecasts typically cover the next five years). Also related to horizon, there are models (e.g. reverse optimizing the market portfolio) that incorporate information about all possible time horizons that would mis-serve us as we try to isolate just the 10-year and longer horizon.

Second, we have avoided so-called "structured" models (e.g. APT, shrinkage, etc.). In Chapter 1, we reviewed the virtues of adding structure to our estimates in the form of ML and Bayesian models to gain accuracy at the expense of introducing bias into our estimates (see Figure 1.6). For example, rather than just using historical distributions, we could have assumed a functional form for our return distributions and their interaction, to account for both heavy tails and non-linear comovement. This assumption would potentially improve our estimation error, but it would introduce additional mathematical complexity and force a specific return distribution into our assumptions. For conceptual simplicity, and to avoid approximation error associated with assuming specific distributional forms, we have avoided imposing structure into our estimation process. There are also equilibrium models (e.g. CAPM, reverse optimization of the global market portfolio, etc.) but these have their own issues. For example, reverse optimizing a market portfolio requires a number of assumptions whose validity we cannot necessarily confirm, such as how different investors model markets, how liquidity needs affect their allocations, how taxes affect their allocations, and so on. Hence, these models introduce other estimation errors we steer clear of in favor of more transparent estimation headwinds.

Our goal is a modern yet practical asset allocation process, and hopefully by the end of this chapter you will be left with a forecasting toolkit that fulfills both goals. Before we dive in, let me preface everything we are about to do with the simple disclaimer that all estimation has error bars, and the entire intent here is to provide something with strong foundational underpinnings and transparent error bars, not a holy grail with perfect accuracy.

USING HISTORY AS OUR FORECAST

Background

We have two requirements for the historical monthly return distribution to be a useful long-horizon forecast: (1) we have enough data to be able to make an accurate assessment of the assets we are investing in; and (2) our assets must be stationary over long periods. Let's first refine our understanding of these requirements with a quick detour on "stochastic processes." This explanation will help the reader build confidence in the systematic process we are building here.

The basic assumption behind using the historical joint return distribution of financial assets as a forecast is that the monthly returns are created by a well-defined stochastic process that repeats, and as long as we can measure it enough times we can get a solid grasp of the process's character. Let's carefully dissect this sentence.

A stochastic process is something that creates the random outcomes observed. In this case, the process is human beings investing in financial markets, and the outcomes are the joint monthly returns of said financial assets. Every day humans buy and sell these assets, and if their behavior and the world they live in don't change too much, then the process that defines monthly returns should be stable in time. So, unless something dramatic happens in our world, such as wild inflation or major tax code changes, the appeal and motivation of buying and selling financial assets will stay constant and the stochastic process can be treated as "stationary," or stable in time.

What exactly does *stable* mean in this context? It simply means that the precise form of the joint return distribution is the same from one era (of a few decades) to the next. We all know return distributions over short and even intermediate term horizons can be very different, but we are focused on horizons greater than 10 years; hence, momentum and mean reversion effects should not get in our way when it comes to stationarity.

Assuming our underlying process is stable, we can conclude that the historical distribution we have observed is just a sample of the process's true distribution, meaning that our historical data points are just a random selection of the possible outcomes that the process can ultimately generate. From Stats 101, we know that when we use a sample to represent a true distribution, there are error bars on our estimates, formally known as the "standard error" by statisticians. This error gets smaller as we increase the sample size, eventually approaching zero as our sample size goes to infinity, giving us a perfect portrayal of the process through its observed outcomes.

In our returns-based optimization framework we are not estimating moments, though. Rather, we are using the entire distribution as the input to our optimizer. So, what exactly would we measure error bars on? Even though we deploy the full return distribution as our forecast, we still have implied estimates of all the distribution's moments that are being utilized by the optimizer. Recall from Chapter 1 that we can fully specify any distribution by an infinite set of moments. Hence, we can analyze the standard errors of the implied moments to assess whether we have enough data for our historical distribution to be a good estimate of the true distribution to present to the optimizer.[1]

With our refined understanding of stochastic processes, and how simple assumptions like stationarity and large sample size can assist us in forecasting, let's now turn to our first key requirement: large sample sizes.

Estimation Error and Sample Size

How do we measure the standard error? Many of you have probably seen an analytic formula for the standard error of a mean estimated from a distribution of $\sigma/\sqrt{T}$ where σ is the volatility of the sample and T is the number of data points. Analytic estimates of this type are available for higher moments as well, but the derivation of these formulas generally requires making assumptions about the type of distribution the data comes from (Wright & Herrington, 2011). For example, the standard error of the mean just reviewed assumes a normal underlying distribution. Given our penchant to avoid parametric estimation methods, where we have to define the functional form of the distribution, we will be avoiding analytic formulas for standard errors.

Instead, we will deploy a bootstrap, one of the most beautiful statistical tools out there, which will be invaluable not just here, but also in Chapter 5 when we study the accuracy of our optimizer-recommended portfolios. Rather than use the entire sample to estimate a moment, a bootstrap uses a random sample of the full dataset to estimate the moment and then repeats that process multiple times to create a distribution of the estimate itself. The standard deviation of that distribution is then the standard error for the estimate. So, we create a number of estimates by randomly sampling our data to see how much those estimates vary—an intuitive means of assessing the accuracy of our estimate. Let's go through an example to flesh out all the details of deploying a bootstrap for calculating standard errors.

Say we have monthly returns for US equities from 1972–2018, giving us 564 data points.[2] Instead of just creating a mean estimate from those 564 data points, we want to create 1,000 different estimates, where each estimate also utilizes 564 data points; but those data points are randomly

---

[1] We will only analyze standard errors of moments of individual asset distributions, not standard errors of co-moments between assets, as this is considered a topic that is beyond the scope of this book. With that said, the standard errors of our recommended asset allocations presented in Chapter 5 certainly contain that information within them; hence, our framework is not completely ignorant of these errors.

[2] In this example, US equities are represented by the value-weight return of all University of Chicago's Booth School of Business (CRSP®) firms incorporated in the US and listed on the NYSE, AMEX, or NASDAQ that have a CRSP share code of 10 or 11, sourced from Ken French's online library.

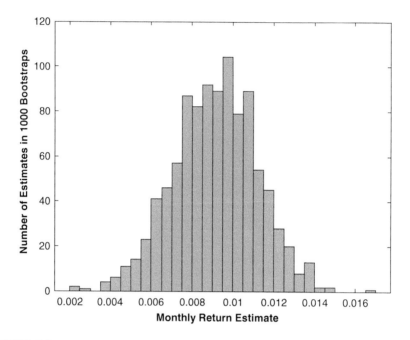

FIGURE 4.1 Bootstrap Estimates of Average Monthly Return for US Equities

sampled. They are not the same as the original set of data points, since we create a new set with replacement—which means if a return is drawn from the original data set, it may be drawn again within the same estimate.

Figure 4.1 shows the distribution of mean estimates from just such a procedure. The mean monthly return estimate from the original 564 data points is 0.0092, which is roughly the center of the distribution in Figure 4.1; however, now we have a distribution of estimates with a clear width. The standard error is then the standard deviation of the bootstrap distribution (it is 0.0018 for the specific 1,000 data sets used in this simulation, but because it is random it changes each time we run the bootstrap).

It is instructive now to follow standard practice and convert this standard error to error bars by multiplying the standard error by two and having our error bars be symmetric around the point estimate. Hence, our estimate of the mean monthly return for US equities based on the historical return distribution is $0.92\% \pm 0.36\%$. If we assume that the bootstrapped estimate distribution is normally distributed,[3] we can deploy standard statistical significance tests that imply we can be 95% confident that the

---

[3]I will not be proving that our bootstrap distributions are normally distributed as this is outside the scope of this book.

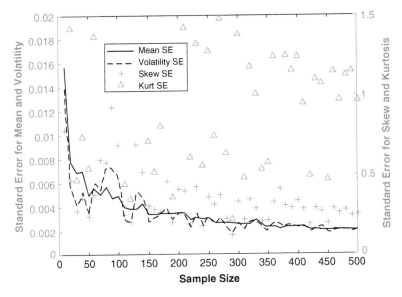

FIGURE 4.2 Standard Error of First Four Moment Estimates for US Equities as a Function of Sample Size

moment we are estimating lies within the error bar range around our estimate.

Figure 4.2 extends this analysis for US equities to the first four moments, and plots the standard error for each moment as a function of sample size, where we vary the sample size of the data being studied backward from the last data point. For example, a sample size of 12 uses data from March 2018 to February 2019, a sample size of 24 uses data from March 2017 to February 2019, and so on. The mean and volatility standard errors are plotted on the left axis while the skew and kurtosis standard errors are plotted on the right axis. Staying focused on the mean standard error for the moment, you can see the standard error drops precipitously as sample size is increased, confirming our assertion that large sample size is paramount for good estimation. And, of course, as our sample size approaches the original 564 used earlier, we see the mean standard error approach our previous result of 0.18%.

Another key observation from Figure 4.2 is that the standard error improvement, once you go beyond 400 samples or so, becomes marginal, a result that is consistent across moments. This leads us to a critical conclusion: using historical data for forecasting should minimally include around 30 years of data but going beyond 50 or so is not overwhelmingly valuable, since standard errors barely improve for each decade added, and we simultaneously include potentially irrelevant data from periods of time unlike that of the current markets.[4] Also apparent in Figure 4.2 is that our higher moment standard errors seem to take a bit longer to reach a steady state value. Hence, for improved higher moment accuracy we should really be pushing our sample size to 40–50 years, instead of just 30 years.

In case you haven't noticed, let me say that we are in a bit of a pickle. Our US equity mean estimate (0.92% ± 0.36%) has sizable error bars that we cannot improve upon by extending our data further back, because we would start to utilize data that was most certainly driven by a different process than it is today (and data isn't even available for most financial assets more than a few decades back). I would assert, though, that while our mean estimate for US equities has sizable error bars, it still paints a clear picture that an equity risk premium exists[5] and should be something we pursue for our clients, especially given the simple fact that we have many credible a priori theoretical reasons for these moments to be significant. Hence, we can have greater conviction that we are simply in a tight spot because of data limitations. In the world of noisy estimation of economically and behaviorally motivated processes with limited data, we are actually doing fine with these error bars.[6] And for all those dogmatic practitioners out there who say historical estimates are useless unless you have hundreds of years of data (indeed, needed, if you want, say, ±1% error bars on annualized equity return forecasts), please step up and show me a model you have with better error bars.[7] And yes, this same logic applies to our noisy estimates of skew and kurtosis as well.

Don't forget that our approach to handle estimation error was not just to minimize estimation error but also to carefully minimize our framework's

---

[4]This is not to say that we would make the same assertion 50 years from now about today. Markets before 1970 look nothing like markets today (consider, for example, the Federal Reserve's updated operating procedures, the end of Bretton Woods, globalization and improved liquidity of financial markets, new financial products, and so on). But the same may not be true of the future relative to today.

[5]The error bars we have in this case, though wide, are indeed tight enough to pass the standard statistics test, where they don't overlap with a "null" estimate of 0. The same applies to our estimates of skew and kurtosis where the null hypothesis is skew of 0 and kurtosis of 3.

[6]We are in a similar situation with estimates of skew, but less so with kurtosis, and even less so with volatility (as reviewed shortly).

[7]To be clear, this challenge to my peers is squarely focused on the error bars of our estimation of the true distribution of a stochastic process; we are not analyzing out-of-sample forecast accuracy. These are two distinct types of errors, and I am only focused on the former here. While out-of-sample accuracy is the goal of deploying estimates of stationary returns with minimal error bars, it is not something we are testing explicitly.

sensitivity to estimation error. Hence, shrinking our error bars is not the only tool we have to combat estimation error. Chapter 3 had us very focused on only investing in assets that were very distinct. Motivated by the fact that our forecasting error bars are indeed larger than we would like, we need to be sure we are not investing in assets that are similar enough to require very precise estimates (recall Figure 1.5, where 1% error bars lead to wildly different asset allocations). Ultimately, the key lesson here is to always try to deploy around 50 years of historical data as the starting point for your joint distribution forecasts, and minimize the number of closely related assets in your portfolio to minimize the effects of the large error bars contained within the forecast distribution.

Is there any way for us to get more comfortable with the error bars we are sitting with? Potentially. It is well known that the estimation of a distribution via historical data is sensitive to outliers. Figure 4.3 plots the same bootstrap exercise we just went through to find standard errors for our first four moments, but with one key difference: we have removed the most extreme positive and negative monthly returns from the dataset (a total of two data points out of 564). As you can see, the standard errors shrink by "winsorizing" just the top and bottom data points, where the effect is exaggerated as we go to higher and higher moments. But these smaller error

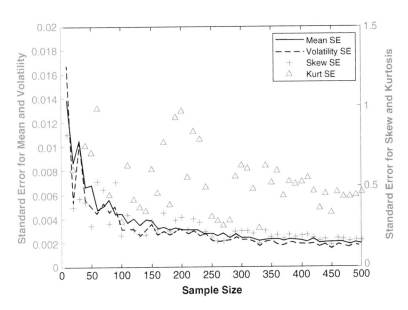

FIGURE 4.3 Standard Error of First Four Moment Estimates for US Equities as a Function of Sample Size after Lowest and Highest Historical Returns Removed

bars should only increase our confidence in our estimation process if the estimate itself did not change too much as a result of truncating the data set. If winsorization changes our estimate significantly, then we are not discovering an extraneous cause of wide error bars; rather, we are modifying the distribution with the uninteresting side-effect of modifying the error bars.

Let's take the kurtosis standard error as an example. The full sample kurtosis estimate is 5.2, with a standard error of approximately 1 when deploying a sample size of 500. But when we remove the highest and lowest data points, this estimate drops to 4 with a standard error near 0.5. Given a kurtosis of 3 for normal distributions, if we were testing how well we have isolated an estimate for a non-normal distribution via the kurtosis score, our estimate of 5 had error bars of ±2 while our estimate of 4 had error bars of ±1. Hence, both give similar confidence in the estimate relative to the "null" assumption of a normal distribution (95% confidence for non-normality). But ultimately the winsorization process has shifted our kurtosis estimate; hence, we cannot rely on the narrower error bars post-winsorization to assuage our concerns with the original error bars.

Lastly, let me point out a peculiar result: the absolute size of the error bars on the volatility and mean are nearly identical while the volatility estimate is about four times larger than the mean estimate. Hence, on a relative basis we have much better accuracy on the volatility estimate than we do on the mean estimate.[8] This well-known artifact of statistical estimation is an important reason why risk-based asset allocation systems have become so popular, especially by those practitioners who use 20 years or less of historical data to estimate moments of a standard mean-variance optimization, where the error bars on the return estimate are overwhelming. This is also a key reason why practitioners are so focused on return estimates beyond historical estimates, but they generally leave volatility forecasting to the purview of historical estimation.

Hopefully, the reader has been imparted enough background on standard errors, sample sizes, and outliers to intelligently assess whether the historical distribution they are looking to use as a forecast for their assets is sufficient for reasonable forecasting from an estimation error standpoint. The key takeaway here is that one should look to use at least 40 years of data when using the returns-based framework laid out in this book, and should

---

[8]For a normal distribution, which we will use here as an analytically solvable example, the standard error of the mean is $\sigma/\sqrt{T}$ while the standard error of the volatility is $\sigma/\sqrt{2T}$; hence, the volatility estimate error bar is lower by $\sqrt{2}$ while the estimated monthly parameter is around four times the size, improving error bars relative to the mean by $4\sqrt{2}$.

always try to minimize the headwinds faced by estimation error by avoiding similar assets whose estimates would need tight error bars to be significantly distinguishable.

Stationarity: Does History Repeat?

The second key requirement for us to confidently deploy historical distributions as forecasts is for the stochastic process that generates the return distribution to be the same throughout time. In statistics, this is referred to as stationarity, or being stationary. Of course, we know return distributions over short- and intermediate-term horizons can be very different, but we are focused on horizons greater than 10 years; hence we care about return distributions being stable over many decades. So, what we want to do is test whether the return distribution of an asset from one era (of a few decades) looks similar to the return distribution of the subsequent era. To this end, all one needs to do is take our 50 years of sample data for each asset and just divide it into two halves and literally compare the distributions. If the distributions are similar, we are all set.

One could certainly try do this by eye, but a much quicker and more foolproof method is to deploy a well-known statistical test called the Kolmogorov–Smirnov (KS) test. This test literally measures the discrepancy between the two distributions for us, by summing up the difference between the number of events at each monthly return level and evaluating whether that difference is enough to say that our return distributions are not a product of the same stochastic process.[9] The result of the test is a simple "Yes" or "No" answer to whether the distribution is stationary: we want yes answers across the board for us to feel good about our assumption that history repeats itself over long horizons.

Figure 4.4 shows the KS test results for the set of asset classes we selected in Chapter 3, ignoring the GRP components for simplicity of presentation. As you can see, for the almost 50 years of data used, the two halves of our samples are flagged as equivalent for equities, real estate, and duration,

---

[9]Similar to our pursuit of 95% confidence levels for our moment estimation error bars in the last section, here we pursue a test with a 5% (1 − 95%) statistical significance level, which represents the probability of rejecting the null hypothesis that the distributions are identical inaccurately (i.e. getting a false negative from the test). Since this test assumes stationarity as its null hypothesis, we are testing the less stringent question of whether the two distributions are clearly not the same, rather than testing whether they are clearly the same. Therefore, this test is more of an "innocent until proven guilty test"—a bit less convincing than the reverse test, for which I do not have a good metric.

	Stationary?	Reason If Not
Equities - Domestic - Div. LO ARP	Yes	-
Real Estate - Domestic - Passive	Yes	-
Duration - Domestic - Passive	Yes	-
Commodities - Passive	No	Outliers
Equities - Domestic - Div. l/s ARP	No	Rate Regime

FIGURE 4.4   Stationarity Test Results (historical data from 1972 to 2018)[10]

but not commodities or our l/s equity ARP. This analysis is then telling us that for the last two assets we cannot expect history to repeat; hence, the historical distribution would be a poor forecast of the future. But before we throw in the hat, there are two circumstances we must account for to be sure our stochastic processes are not stable over longer periods.

The first is showcased in the case of commodities and has to do with the effect of outliers. If we remove a handful of outliers, the test actually flips to a confirming "Yes," giving us renewed solace that the two distributions are indeed not too far off. Only a handful of extreme instances greatly distort the test, which is indeed not very many over an almost 50-year history.[11] But could those outlying data points be legitimate defining features of our asset class? In this instance, the kurtosis (but not the first three moments) of commodities when winsorized changes dramatically; hence we cannot just simply leverage the winsorized data set as a forecast. But, what really matters regarding deploying winsorized data as a forecast is whether the winsorization affects the results of the optimizer. As discussed in Chapter 1, and validated in Chapter 5 for one specific set of asset classes, of our four moments, kurtosis has by far the least impact on optimizers, given its fourth order nature (see Eq. (1.4)). Hence, given the lack of distortion to the first

---

[10]Treasuries are represented by constant maturity indices from the Center for Research in Security Prices at the University of Chicago's Booth School of Business (CRSP®); equity data is from Ken French's online library with all factor assets following conventional definitions; real estate is represented by the FTSE Nareit US Real Estate Index; and commodities are expressed via the S&P GSCI Commodity Index.
[11]The Kolmogorov–Smirnov test, similar to other significance tests like the Jarque–Bera test from Chapter 1, will never reject the null hypothesis when the sample size is small, due to the test's low conviction by virtue of the limited number of data points (and not based on the thing we are actually trying to test for). So, users beware when small sample sizes are flagged as stationary.

three moments when winsorizing commodities, and the minimal effect the fourth moment has during optimization of our current asset class configuration, we can use the winsorized commodities data as a forecast and have reasonable stationarity. And the easiest way to confirm that winsorization doesn't affect our optimization process is simply to run the optimizer, with and without winsorization, and look for any discrepancies in the outputs.

The second situation we must account for in this analysis, on display in our l/s asset class, is the effect of secular shifts in the mean return. If we adjust up the mean of the monthly return distribution for the second half of data by 0.1% (i.e. add 10bps of return to every single monthly return in the second half of our sample), the KS test flips to "Yes" for the l/s asset class. Hence, it looks like there was a secular shift in the mean return between the first half of our approximately 50-year period and the second half. But we know that interest rates, a potentially key driver of l/s strategy returns, have shifted lower from the 1970s and 1980s to now, which could certainly shift the mean return of the distribution down from the first half to the second half of our sample. For instance, we would certainly expect value to fare worse than growth in a low rate environment as growth stocks can be supported by low funding costs. This interest rate regime shift is certainly seen in other asset classes, and should always be accounted for in our forecasts, but it is only currently flagged by our KS test for l/s ARP, and not in, say, US equities or duration. This is because the l/s ARP is starting with a mean monthly return that is about one-third the size of US equities and one-half the size of our 30-year Treasury asset, creating a much larger sensitivity within the test to the background rate shift for our l/s ARP asset. In summary, if an asset is stationary withstanding secular mean return shifts, one should feel comfortable that the stochastic process is stable but the forecasted monthly return should be shifted if the most recent secular trend is not expected to continue.

We just shifted the mean monthly return of a distribution by adding a constant to the entire time series, but is that a legitimate thing to do to a return distribution? And what about accounting for things like fees and taxes in our return distributions? It is now time to review how historical return distributions can be modified to create custom forecasts, and to delineate clearly the primary types of adjustments one needs to be concerned with in the long-term asset allocation problem.

ADJUSTING FORECASTS

Pre-Tax Adjustments

The reader is hopefully now comfortable with using a substantial historical data set, when stationarity can be verified, as a sound forecast for the entire distribution of future outcomes. But what if we want to alter those forecasts for upcoming secular shifts, as we saw was necessary in the case of assets dominated by the background interest rate regime? In that instance, we simply shifted the mean monthly return by adding a constant to each monthly data point. But what about manipulating our forecasts for other situations? How does this work when our forecast is an entire return distribution, where we no longer have individual moment forecasts to manipulate? Are we going to need to modify the distribution point-by-point (i.e. month-by-month)? The answer is thankfully no.

Modifying a historical return distribution forecast could theoretically be done at the monthly data-point level, but given the types of adjustments we would want to make to our history-based forecast, we will not have to manipulate individual outcomes. Given our long-term focus here, Figure 4.5 outlines the full list of possible circumstances one may want to adjust history for. The great news about this list is that every single one of these circumstances (except capital gains taxes, which we will tackle in the next section) can be accounted for in our return distribution forecast by simply adding a constant to each monthly return, just as we did in the last section regarding a secular market shift in interest rates. Hence, we do not need to adjust forecasts on a month-by-month basis.

It is important to note that adding a constant to each data point in a return distribution doesn't affect any higher moments. Our simple shifting system is cleanly modifying return forecasts, without interfering with any other distribution characteristics. In my opinion, this is one of the most attractive parts of deploying a framework that utilizes the entire return distribution. Most modifications you want to make to historical returns to refine your forecast are just return adjustments, which can be made via simple addition and do not have any unwanted effects on higher moments. Let's now quickly go through each category listed in Figure 4.5 not covered thus far to ensure we have a thorough understanding of each type of modification.

Management fees are deducted regularly from performance, and thus behave precisely like a simple shift in monthly returns; so, deploying a return distribution shift for this purpose should be rather intuitive. With that said,

Pre-Tax	Post-Tax
Secular Market Shifts	Qualified Dividends
Management Fees	Unqualified Dividends
Manager Alpha	Long-Term Capital Gains

FIGURE 4.5   Reasons to Modify Historical Estimates

this simple system does not extend to the case of performance fees, which do not get debited like clockwork from the client's account as management fees do. That's fine for our current use case, since we are solely focused on liquid investment vehicles (it is typically illiquid investments that charge performance fees).

Manager alpha is the most subtle category on the left side of Figure 4.5, given the fact that every manager is different in the value they add to the passive benchmarks this book is focused on. However, here we assume that manager alpha is indeed alpha to the benchmark in the purest sense (leftover return in a regression against the benchmark when the regression coefficient is 1). In that context, manager alpha can indeed be accounted for via a mean monthly return shift. But be warned that if you have a manager due diligence process, and you want to account for your manager's skill (e.g. skill in mispricing, timing, or control) solely via a simple mean shift in the forecast distribution of the core asset class, be sure that your manager is not doing anything to change the shape of the return distribution relative to his benchmark, and is only shifting the distribution. The easiest way to check this is to use the moment contribution tool from Chapter 3, and precisely assess whether your manager is adding alpha or is introducing an unwanted higher moment relative to the passive benchmark. Though our discussion of moment contributions in Chapter 3 was focused on asset classes, there is no reason we couldn't use that framework as a valuable due diligence tool to assess both the magnitude of the alpha that managers provide and whether they are changing the distribution beyond just a simple shift.

Post-Tax Adjustments

The first two type of taxes in Figure 4.5, qualified and unqualified dividends, are also accounted for by the simple performance shift we have been focused on thus far. This should be clear by realizing that dividends are regular payouts that are always expected to happen, the tax on which is then just a regular debit from our return stream; so, they can be accounted for by shifting monthly returns by a constant.

The last category in Figure 4.5, capital gains, is more complicated to handle than with a simple return shift. If we assume that a realized loss can offset income somewhere else, then capital gains taxes actually reduce the magnitude of your losses just as much as they reduce your gains. Thus, capital gains tax actually mutes both losses and gains in your distribution symmetrically, which we can account for by multiplying (AKA scaling) all the monthly returns by a constant less than 1. So yes, in addition to lowering the mean return by the capital gains tax rate, capital gains taxes also lower the volatility of the asset under consideration, an artifact many refer to as the government acting as a risk-sharing partner (Wilcox, Horvitz, & diBartolomeo, 2006).

The easiest way to think of this risk-sharing partnership we have with the government is as follows. When you have capital losses, you get to offset them against other income or capital gains, lowering your realized loss while the government simultaneously loses the taxable gains that you just offset with your losses. This lowers the cashflow seen by the government, exposing them to the downside of your portfolio; thus, the government is sharing your risks.

The process for scaling a return distribution is simple when all we have is an asset with 100% realized capital gains (where there are no unrealized gains and no dividends). We simply multiply each monthly return by (1 − capital gains tax rate). For example, a 15% long-term capital gains tax rate would have us scaling our returns by 0.85. In truth, real-world situations are typically more complex, as there are income components to the total return and not all gains are fully realized. In the most general case, the capital gains tax scaling factor applied to the return distribution after all other return distribution shifts (pre-tax and dividends) have already been made is

Equation 4.1 Capital Gains Tax Scaling Factor

$$Capital\ Gains\ Tax\ Scaling\ Factor = 1 - \frac{Total\ Capital\ Gains\ Tax}{Post - Dividend\ Tax\ Total\ Return}$$

where the total capital gains tax is just pre-tax price appreciation * turnover * capital gains tax rate, turnover is the fraction of capital gains realized (ranges from 0 to 100%), and the post-dividend tax total return is the total return after dividend taxes have been removed (this is our normalization since we are applying the scaling on that precise return distribution). As you can see, if turnover is 100% and all returns are in the form of price appreciation, then you recover our earlier formula of (1 − capital gains tax rate). Let me reiterate that this formula is premised on the fact that we will sequentially alter our return distributions in the following order: first pre-tax shifts, then post-dividend tax shifts, and finally post-capital gains tax scaling. This order is important, since we must scale our historical returns for capital gains taxes only after they have been adjusted first for performance shifts and then additionally by dividend tax drags.

Figure 4.6 takes the reader through the full process, step by step, for adjusting the return distribution of US equities for both pre-tax and post-tax adjustments, where this example is all carried out in annualized terms for

Step 1: Pre-Tax Adjustment

1A. Historical Mean	7.00%
1B. Secular Market Shift	0.00%
1C. Management Fees	−0.40%
1D. Manager Alpha	1.20%
1E. Pre-Tax Shift	0.80%
1F. Pre-Tax Total Return	7.80%

Step 2: Post-Tax Adjustment (Dividends)

2A. Qualified Dividend yield	1.00%
2B. Qualified Dividend Tax Rate	15.00%
2C. Unqualified Dividend yield	1.00%
2D. Unqualified Dividend Tax Rate	35.00%
2E. Post-Dividend Tax Shift	−0.500%
2F. Post-Dividend Tax Total Return	7.30%

Step 3: Post-Tax Adjustment (Capital Gains)

3A. Pre-Tax Price Appreciation	5.80%	3D. Total Capital Gains Tax	0.087%
3B. Turnover	10.00%	3E. Effective Capital Gains Tax Rate = Total Capital Gains Tax/Post-Dividend Tax Total Return	1.2%
3C. Capital Gains Tax Rate	15.00%	3F. Capital Gains Scaling = 1-Effective Capital Gains Tax Rate	0.988

FIGURE 4.6 Calculation Steps for Return Distribution Shifting and Scaling

ease (the monthly return shift is just the annual return shift divided by 12, whereas the monthly return scaling is the same as the annualized version).

Since taxes are applied at the gross performance level, one begins by first making all pre-tax adjustments, and then applying tax shifts afterwards. In steps 1A to 1F in Figure 4.6, we first shift the return distribution by 80bps (1E), given our expectations that our manager will be able to add 120bps of alpha while only charging a fee of 40bps. We then shift the return distribution by dividend taxes, which includes both qualified and non-qualified dividends that are taxed at different rates, as outlined in steps 2A to 2F. To calculate this shift, we first assess how much return we expect from each dividend type (2A and 2C), then specify the tax rate of each dividend type (2B and 2D). Next, the total tax from each type is subtracted from the pre-tax distribution mean, which is −15bps (1% qualified dividend taxed at 15%) and −35bps (1% unqualified dividend taxed at 35%), for a grand total of a −50bps shift (2E). Finally, we must calculate the scaling of the post-dividend tax adjusted distribution based on our capital gains expectations, as reviewed in steps 3A–3F in Figure 4.6.

As outlined in Eq. (4.1), we first need to find our expectation for pre-tax price appreciation, achieved by taking the shifted pre-tax return expectation and subtracting the pre-tax return of the dividends, in this case 5.8% (7% + 80bps −1% − 1%). We then multiply this 5.8% by the turnover we expect in the asset class, since only those positions actually sold are taxed. Turnover is 10% in this instance, giving us 58bps of realized capital gains. The taxes on this amount, at a rate of 15%, is then 8.7bps, which is the total capital gains tax. The capital gains scaling parameter for US equities, which we multiply by the post-dividend tax adjusted return stream, is then just 1 − .087%/7.3% = .988 (3F).

Now that we have a customizable joint return distribution forecast, backed by transparent and defensible principles from stochastic calculus and statistics, it is time to bring together everything we have laid out thus far in the book, and finally run an optimizer to create our client portfolios.

5

Portfolio Optimization

Step 4 of four in our asset allocation process brings us to our crowning moment: running an optimizer to produce portfolios that respect nuanced client preferences while simultaneously being robust to estimation error. The chapter begins with a review of our optimizer results as a function of our three-dimensional client risk profile space, showcasing an intuitive evolution of portfolios as our three preference parameters change. We then spend time contrasting our framework with other potential solutions to elucidate the value of our three-dimensional risk preference utility functions. The chapter ends with a review of the sensitivity of our recommended portfolios to estimation error, as we deploy the bootstrap method to create error bars on each asset's recommended allocation.

Key Takeaways:

1. Our modern utility function results in an intuitive three-dimensional landscape of optimized portfolios that is rich in behavioral content.
2. The three-dimensional utility function is a critical requirement for systematic incorporation of financial goals into a PT-conscious asset allocation framework, even when higher moments are not meaningful.
3. The error bars on our optimizer's recommended portfolio allocations are large but manageable, highlighting the importance of always minimizing estimation error and its consequences.
4. Our asset allocation error bars go down as we expand our outcome forecasting sample size, and as we limit redundancy of asset classes, validating our deployment of these techniques for this purpose.

INTRODUCTION

This book has promised a modern yet practical solution to the asset allocation problem within wealth management. On the modern side, we promised an advanced client profile, defined by a utility function with three risk pref-erence parameters, and an intelligent balance sheet moderation system of these preferences. On this front, we also deployed a returns-based expected utility optimization routine that can account for higher order moments of the assets we invest in. On the practical side, we promised a solution with reasonable estimation error and lower estimation error sensitivity. To this end, we deployed non-parametric estimation from historical data with large sample sizes, alongside an asset selection process that minimizes estimation error sensitivity by avoiding redundant assets, so that our optimizer could be run without unnecessary sensitivity to inputs or manually imposed allo-cation constraints. It is now time to run our optimizer and see if the pieces we have put in place result in an investment solution that delivers on our promises.

The chapter begins with a review of the portfolios recommended by our modern utility function. We will see an intuitive evolution of risk-taking as we traverse the three-dimensional space defined by the three risk behaviors we are accounting for. We then compare our framework with other possible solutions to drive home the key benefits of our modernized three-dimensional risk profile system: a client profile rich in intuitive behav-ioral content, and the ability to incorporate financial goals systematically when human behavior is properly accounted for.

We then move on to the practical side of our framework, designed to address the challenges of optimizer sensitivity, which pushes many advisors away from using optimizers and into generic heuristic methods. We will deploy the bootstrap method once again, this time sampling with replace-ment from the full history of joint distributions when feeding outcomes into our optimizer. This creates error bars on our recommended asset allocation results that will help inform whether our framework is indeed helping reduce estimation error and the sensitivity to it. We will see our recommended techniques of deploying assets with low mimicking portfolio tracking error (MPTE) and large sample size successfully help us improve our asset alloca-tion error bars.

OPTIMIZATION RESULTS

Figure 5.1 shows our returns-based optimization results for our chosen asset classes (for simplicity, without our equity and duration geographic risk pre-mium (GRP)). We deploy our full 1972–2018 joint return distribution as our forecast, with no tax, fee, or other adjustments, and only show a subset

φ = 0, λ = 1

Asset	γ = 3	γ = 6	γ = 12
Equities - Domestic - Div. LO ARP	81%	53%	33%
Real Estate - Domestic - Passive	0%	0%	0%
Duration - Domestic - Passive	19%	38%	30%
Commodities - Passive	0%	9%	9%
Equities - Domestic - Div. I/s ARP	0%	0%	28%

φ = 1, λ = 1

Asset	γ = 3	γ = 6	γ = 12
Equities - Domestic - Div. LO ARP	100%	100%	100%
Real Estate - Domestic - Passive	0%	0%	0%
Duration - Domestic - Passive	0%	0%	0%
Commodities - Passive	0%	0%	0%
Equities - Domestic - Div. I/s ARP	0%	0%	0%

φ = 0, λ = 1.5

Asset	γ = 3	γ = 6	γ = 12
Equities - Domestic - Div. LO ARP	38%	30%	24%
Real Estate - Domestic - Passive	0%	0%	0%
Duration - Domestic - Passive	34%	28%	24%
Commodities - Passive	9%	8%	8%
Equities - Domestic - Div. I/s ARP	19%	34%	44%

φ = 1, λ = 1.5

Asset	γ = 3	γ = 6	γ = 12
Equities - Domestic - Div. LO ARP	53%	51%	50%
Real Estate - Domestic - Passive	1%	3%	11%
Duration - Domestic - Passive	35%	33%	25%
Commodities - Passive	11%	13%	14%
Equities - Domestic - Div. I/s ARP	0%	0%	0%

φ = 0, λ = 3

Asset	γ = 3	γ = 6	γ = 12
Equities - Domestic - Div. LO ARP	20%	19%	18%
Real Estate - Domestic - Passive	0%	0%	0%
Duration - Domestic - Passive	20%	20%	19%
Commodities - Passive	6%	6%	6%
Equities - Domestic - Div. I/s ARP	54%	55%	57%

φ = 1, λ = 3

Asset	γ = 3	γ = 6	γ = 12
Equities - Domestic - Div. LO ARP	21%	21%	21%
Real Estate - Domestic - Passive	0%	0%	0%
Duration - Domestic - Passive	21%	20%	20%
Commodities - Passive	6%	6%	7%
Equities - Domestic - Div. I/s ARP	52%	53%	52%

FIGURE 5.1 Optimization Results for Selected γ, λ, and φ

of γ and λ values, again in an effort to keep the presentation simple.[1] There are four key takeaways the reader should glean from the menu of portfolios in Figure 5.1, which should both validate the framework we have developed in this book and provide refined intuition for how the framework can be deployed across a wide client base.

First, the resulting portfolios demonstrate an intuitive evolution of portfolios as we navigate through the three-dimensional space of client risk parameters. Higher risk aversion, higher loss aversion, and lower reflection all lead to portfolios with lower allocations to performance assets and higher allocations to diversifying assets. If this flow of portfolios is not intuitive at this point, I recommend going back to Figure 1.4 and spending some time to connect rigorously the utility function shape to an optimizer's decision. In a nutshell: higher risk aversion and loss aversion both create a utility function that drops off in the loss domain more precipitously,

---

[1]Treasuries are represented by constant maturity indices from the Center for Research in Security Prices at the University of Chicago's Booth School of Business (CRSP®); equity data is from Ken French's online library with all factor assets following conventional definitions; real estate is represented by the FTSE Nareit US Real Estate Index; and commodities are expressed via the S&P GSCI Commodity Index.

pushing the optimizer away from assets with more outcomes in the extreme loss domain (due to high volatility, negative skew, etc.), while reflection of 1 causes utility in the loss domain to curve up, pushing the optimizer toward performance assets once again.

Second, Figure 5.1 showcases an incredible amount of variation in the portfolios as we change our three parameters, especially as we expand beyond our neoclassical parameter γ and vary our two behavioral parameters λ and φ. This variation helps validate the value of accounting for these two additional dimensions of risk preferences, since their effects are indeed not marginal. For instance, comparing a $\gamma = 3$ and $\varphi = 0$ portfolio, for $\lambda = 1$ and $\lambda = 3$, we see a shift in equity allocation of over 60%. This is a huge difference, which begs the obvious question: Are advisors who don't account for loss aversion and reflection potentially misallocating by 60%? The answer is yes, advisors could potentially be that far off, and this could have played a big role behind the struggles advisors encountered with many clients during and immediately after the Great Recession, where portfolios turned in larger drawdowns than were acceptable by clients. The precise answer to this question depends on how advisors are measuring risk aversion in the modern portfolio theory (MPT) setting, and it requires some careful elaboration. See the next section, where we carefully examine this question.

Pulling this thread just one step further before we move on, Figure 5.1 also showcases some powerful nuances regarding how the three-dimensional portfolio map evolves. We see that λ is the most dominant of the three risk preference parameters, in the sense that changing φ or γ has little effect on recommended portfolios, as λ increases. For example, look how much the portfolios vary as you change γ when $\lambda = 1$ and $\varphi = 0$ while there's basically no variation as you change γ when $\lambda = 3$ and $\varphi = 0$. We also see that φ takes second place in terms of which parameters have the most influence on our portfolios: we see plenty of variation with γ when $\lambda = 1$ and $\varphi = 0$ but zero variation as you change γ when $\lambda = 1$ and $\varphi = 1$. λ's dominance over φ when λ deviates from 1 is also brightly on display, as one sees only marginal differences between the portfolios for $\varphi = 0$ and $\varphi = 1$ when $\lambda = 3$. This clear domination of λ and φ over γ should hopefully add to your conviction that these components of human behavior shouldn't be ignored when accurately mapping client preferences to portfolios. This is another great time to reflect back on Figure 1.4 and see if this order of dominance is intuitive given what we know about our utility function as parameters evolve. When I personally look at Figure 1.4, it is rather intuitive that λ and φ would dominate γ, given the contrast between the slow shift of the power utility curvature as γ is changed to the rapid shift in utility shape that occurs when λ or φ change.

Third, the evolution of the portfolios seen in Figure 5.1 as parameters are changed is generally smooth, an important feature of a robust asset allocation framework. And we are skipping some values we would like to distinguish (as set out in Chapter 2) in this presentation, for simplicity; so, the portfolio transitions are in fact even smoother than what is pictured. Up to now, this book has solely focused on the robustness of recommended asset allocations with regard to the asset classes chosen and the capital market assumptions deployed, but here we are talking about robustness to a different set of variables: our three-dimensional risk profile variables. If our framework varied wildly with just minor changes to our profile parameters, we would have a robustness challenge with respect to those variables; so it is nice to see a generally well-behaved set of output portfolios as our three risk parameters evolve.

And fourth, Figure 5.1 shows a strong preference for the long/short (l/s) asset class when λ gets high. As discussed in Chapter 3, the l/s asset class reduces volatility faster than duration at the expense of mean, skew, and kurtosis detraction. And it is clear that the optimizer will accept all three of those detractive moment contributions in exchange for lower volatility as aversion to risk and loss increases. But hold on! A highly asymmetric utility function (e.g. $\varphi = 0$ and $\lambda = 3$) is showing strong focus on minimizing the second moment without much regard to third or higher moments—exactly the situation where one may expect our utility to have heightened focus on avoiding skew detraction, for instance. Hence, when λ gets high, what we are seeing is not the effect of higher moments being accounted for; rather, we are seeing a client profile with a higher "generalized" risk aversion, which will penalize volatility more heavily during the optimization. So why is the utility function behaving like a mean-variance (M-V) optimizer, without strong focus on increasing skew or lowering kurtosis?

While we justified the moment preferences (higher skew, lower kurtosis, etc.) in Chapter 1 for a kinked utility ($\lambda > 1$ and $\varphi = 0$), we never presented the magnitude of the different order derivatives that acted as the sensitivity setting to each moment (see Eq. (1.4)). It turns out that cranking up the loss aversion in our utility function for the assets deployed here did not ramp up the sensitivity to higher moments enough for us to see a dramatic effect from those moments. And we purposefully deployed distinct assets to minimize estimation error sensitivity; but right when we do that, the means and variances of our assets are going to be wildly different, since these will greatly drive the MPTE decision—given they are first and second order effects, respectively, and ultimately swaping out the higher moments in the optimization decision for all but the most extremely non-normal assets. If instead we were optimizing very similar assets with sizable higher moments (especially those with lower mean and variances, such as hedge funds), the

	$\gamma = 6, \lambda = 1.5, \varphi = 0$	M-V (matched return)	M-Semivar (matched return)
Equities - Domestic - Div. LO ARP	30%	30%	30%
Real Estate - Domestic - Passive	0%	0%	0%
Duration - Domestic - Passive	28%	27%	30%
Commodities - Passive	8%	10%	7%
Equities - Domestic - Div. l/s ARP	34%	33%	33%

FIGURE 5.2 Comparison with Mean-Variance and Mean-Semivariance Frameworks When Returns Are Matched

higher moments would have a much larger effect on the optimizer's decision by virtue of the lower moments being more similar (and smaller).

To demonstrate formally our lack of dependence on higher moments for our current asset list (and underlying capital market assumptions), Figure 5.2 compares optimizer results for our three-dimensional utility function ($\gamma = 6$, $\lambda = 1.5$, and $\varphi = 0$) to the mean-variance and mean-semivariance frameworks for a set return level. Mean-semivariance is just like M-V except it only considers volatility when it is to the downside (AKA semivariance), a simple system for accounting for the intuitive asymmetric preferences toward upside over downside, which we indeed fully capture via λ in our prospect theory utility function. These two additional portfolios in Figure 5.2 have been optimized while holding constant the portfolio return to have the same expected return as our optimized three-dimensional utility portfolio. If our three-dimensional utility function indeed had outsized higher moment sensitivity compared to the two other target functions being optimized, then our three-dimensional utility optimization results would create distinct portfolios from these other methods due to those extra terms. In this case, however, we indeed see virtually equivalent portfolios in Figure 5.2 across the three methods, since our three-dimensional utility has negligible contributions from higher moment terms in this configuration. To be fair, we do see the mean-semivariance portfolio deviating from the mean-variance solution in Figure 5.2 by 3 percentage points; but the magnitude of this deviation is well within our allocation error bars, as reviewed in the last section of this chapter, so we do not flag that difference as very relevant.

With that said, our three-dimensional risk preference utility function is still an invaluable improvement from the traditional approach, as it provides for an insightful mapping of client preferences to portfolios based on real-world behaviors and allows for the systematic moderation of preferences based on client goals. Let's now take some time to refine our understanding of the value proposition of our three-dimensional utility function.

TO MPT OR NOT TO MPT?

Since higher moments have played a minimal role for our current asset configuration, an important question is: Can we pivot back to the MPT formulation? We obviously cannot if higher moments are relevant, which we really don't know unless we go through the full utility function optimization process in the first place. But for argument's sake, let's assume we know a priori that higher moments won't be critical—for instance, if we were always optimizing portfolios with our current five asset classes with the same joint return distribution.

Recall from Eq. (1.4) that the sensitivity of our utility function to the second moment is a function of the second derivative of our function, which is in fact a function of all three of our utility parameters γ, λ, and φ. In the current setting of marginal higher moment sensitivity, we can write our three-dimensional utility function as

Equation 5.1 2nd Order Approximation of Our Three-Dimensional Utility Function

$$U = mean(r) - \frac{\gamma^{gen}}{2} variance(r)$$

where r is the portfolio return and γ^{gen} is a function of γ, λ, and φ. For example, a utility function with very high loss aversion will certainly create strong aversion to volatility; and a utility function with reflection would push aversion to volatility in the opposite direction. Hopefully at this point it is rather intuitive to see how our two behavioral parameters affect γ^{gen}. If it isn't clear, I encourage readers to review Figure 5.1 and the discussion in the previous section.

As already noted, this reduction of the problem to a simple tradeoff between return and risk is on bright display in Figure 5.1. As one prefers less volatility, by virtue of preferring higher γ, higher λ, and no reflection ($\varphi = 0$)—which will all make γ^{gen} go up—one clearly sees a shift to the last three assets, precisely those assets we labeled as "diversifying" in Chapter 3. The most extreme example of this would be the third column of the matrix at the bottom left of Figure 5.1 ($\gamma = 12$, $\lambda = 3$, and $\varphi = 0$) where we see the highest allocation to diversifying assets among all portfolios.

	$\gamma = 6, \lambda = 1.5, \varphi = 0$	M-V $(\gamma = 6)$	M-Semivar $(\gamma = 6)$
Equities - Domestic - Div. LO ARP	30%	54%	76%
Real Estate - Domestic - Passive	0%	0%	0%
Duration - Domestic - Passive	28%	36%	24%
Commodities - Passive	8%	10%	0%
Equities - Domestic - Div. l/s ARP	34%	0%	0%

FIGURE 5.3 Comparison with Mean-Variance and Mean-Semivariance Frameworks

We could justify the need for our additional parameters if we assumed people did not have access to γ^{gen} and could only ascertain γ. Figure 5.3 shows the recommended portfolio deploying three frameworks. The first is our three-dimensional utility function, with $\gamma = 6$, $\lambda = 1.5$, and $\varphi = 0$, the second being mean-variance with $\gamma = 6$, and the third being mean-semivariance with $\gamma = 6$. As you can see, while all these portfolios have $\gamma = 6$, they produce very different portfolios. Hence, a mistaken application of γ in the place of γ^{gen} can lead to very misleading portfolios.[2]

If we are careful though, we should be able to measure γ^{gen} carefully, rather than γ, and we could avoid deploying the wrong optimization coefficient. But once we focus on measuring just γ^{gen} (instead of γ, λ, and φ), we lose an incredible amount of detail about our client that helps build intuition behind our process of building a portfolio for them. In my experience, this information is incredibly well received by the client, as they are generally interested in a more nuanced dissection of their personality rather than an effective representation. The three traits we are dissecting in our three-dimensional risk profile are part of the client's everyday life, and it is precisely that color that clients really appreciate a dialogue in. For instance, loss aversion relates to the type of phone case one buys, or it relates to how much life insurance one would be inclined to buy. It is this kind of information clients really enjoy seeing fleshed out as they gain a nuanced understanding of their own behavior. And it is wonderful to see how quickly the three risk preferences can help a client with daily decisions of all kinds outside the investment portfolio, with the proper education on the subject.

---

[2]We see an even more extreme discrepancy between our 3D utility and mean-semivariance because the risk metric of semivariance is a significantly smaller quantity than the volatility by definition, hence putting less weight on the risk side of the ledger for the optimizer, since it roughly only measures half the distribution width.

In addition, this more detailed personality discovery process generally helps the client validate the advisor's process by demonstrating to them that the traits being diagnosed by the three-dimensional risk profile align with their actual behavior.[3] Hence, the three-dimensional utility measurement process should provide an engaging process for clients with the welcome benefit of validating the advisor's process in the eye of the client.

But here comes the hammer: up to this point in our discussion of approximating our three-dimensional function with γ^{gen}, we have assumed there are no financial goals to be accounted for. In Chapter 2, we introduced a system that moderated our three risk preferences independently based on our client's standard of living risk (SLR). In some configuration of the universe, which is not the one we live in, the three-dimensional parameters' moderation may have been collapsible into a system that is squarely focused on γ^{gen}. But because our goals-based moderations of the three parameters don't all go in the same direction of portfolio volatility, we can't do this. For example, when SLR is high, we are expected to moderate λ down and γ up. But these two moderations push the portfolio in different directions regarding volatility. For example, starting from a portfolio with $\gamma = 6$, $\lambda = 1.5$, and $\varphi = 0$ in Figure 5.1, moderating just risk aversion up lowers portfolio volatility while moderating just loss aversion down increases portfolio volatility. It is thus impossible to properly moderate our three-dimensional risk preferences for financial goals with a single generalized risk aversion coefficient, because one of our two irrational preferences (loss aversion) is moderated toward a higher volatility portfolio, in the opposite direction of our other two parameters.

ASSET ALLOCATION SENSITIVITY

A key criterion for our practical asset allocation framework was to build a system that wouldn't be highly sensitive to changes in the underlying capital market assumptions; otherwise we would require forecasting precision that is out of our reach. Figure 1.5 showcased just how sensitive a portfolio allocation could be with only minimal changes to return expectations if the assets are very similar—precisely the behavior we want to avoid. So, how do we measure this sensitivity without sitting here and constantly rerunning our optimizer with different assumptions to see how much the recommended portfolios change?

---

[3]This client validation process is also one way the author has gained comfort with the questionnaires being deployed in Chapter 2, outside the more formal domain of psychometric testing of validity.

One succinct solution is to deploy the bootstrap method once again, a technique we are now very familiar with after Chapter 4. To recap: we created random samples of the full dataset to estimate the moment of interest and then repeated that process many times to create a distribution of the estimate itself, whose width we used as error bars to our estimate. Here, we are interested in the distribution of each asset's recommended asset allocation; so, we will create a random sample of the joint return distribution input as our optimizer's outcome forecasts, find the optimal portfolios, and then repeat this process many times to find a distribution of the recommended portfolio allocations, creating error bars around our recommended asset allocations.

Figure 5.4 shows the asset allocation results from Figure 5.1 for a single value of risk aversion ($\gamma = 6$), where we have now added our bootstrapped error bars on each asset's recommended allocation, where two striking features stand out. The first is that the error bars are not that small! This may surprise some readers, who have most likely never seen error bars on their asset allocations before; but the results may also be intuitive at this point after our results on moment estimation error from Chapter 4, where our error bars were not as small as we would have liked.

$\varphi = 0$		$\varphi = 1$	
	$\gamma = 6$		$\gamma = 6$
Equities - Domestic - Div. LO ARP	53% ± 26%	Equities - Domestic - Div. LO ARP	100% ± 53%
Real Estate - Domestic - Passive	0% ± 14%	Real Estate - Domestic - Passive	0% ± 44%
$\lambda = 1$ Duration - Domestic - Passive	38% ± 27%	$\lambda = 1$ Duration - Domestic - Passive	0% ± 26%
Commodities - Passive	9% ± 19%	Commodities - Passive	0% ± 19%
Equities - Domestic - Div. I/s ARP	0% ± 22%	Equities - Domestic - Div. I/s ARP	0% ± 0%

$\varphi = 0$		$\varphi = 1$	
	$\gamma = 6$		$\gamma = 6$
Equities - Domestic - Div. LO ARP	30% ± 14%	Equities - Domestic - Div. LO ARP	51% ± 43%
Real Estate - Domestic - Passive	0% ± 7%	Real Estate - Domestic - Passive	3% ± 26%
$\lambda = 1.5$ Duration - Domestic - Passive	28% ± 21%	$\lambda = 1.5$ Duration - Domestic - Passive	33% ± 36%
Commodities - Passive	8% ± 10%	Commodities - Passive	13% ± 18%
Equities - Domestic - Div. I/s ARP	34% ± 28%	Equities - Domestic - Div. I/s ARP	0% ± 18%

$\varphi = 0$		$\varphi = 1$	
	$\gamma = 6$		$\gamma = 6$
Equities - Domestic - Div. LO ARP	19% ± 6%	Equities - Domestic - Div. LO ARP	21% ± 9%
Real Estate - Domestic - Passive	0% ± 3%	Real Estate - Domestic - Passive	0% ± 4%
$\lambda = 3$ Duration - Domestic - Passive	20% ± 9%	$\lambda = 3$ Duration - Domestic - Passive	20% ± 11%
Commodities - Passive	6% ± 4%	Commodities - Passive	6% ± 5%
Equities - Domestic - Div. I/s ARP	55% ± 14%	Equities - Domestic - Div. I/s ARP	53% ± 19%

FIGURE 5.4 Error Bars on Optimization Results for Selected γ, λ, and φ

On this point I would say that, similar to the messaging from Chapter 4 on moment estimation error, in the world of noisy estimation of economically and behaviorally motivated risk premia with limited data, we are actually doing fine with these error bars. The larger takeaway is that we, as fiduciaries, should always be mindful of error bars in our research process. For example, running an optimizer based on very limited historical data would be irresponsible regarding estimation error. Additionally, we should be careful when we split hairs on our client profile buckets. For instance, if you bucket your clients into 100 distinct levels of risk aversion, I would immediately challenge whether your estimation error allows you to distinguish portfolios with that level of accuracy.

The second main takeaway from Figure 5.4 is that the error bars go down as our generalized risk aversion goes up. This makes a lot of sense, since the error bars in the riskier portfolios are predominantly driven by the estimation error associated with the riskier assets, which by their very nature have higher estimation error due to their higher volatility.

In Chapter 3 we saw that, on a percentage basis, the error bars on volatility were much smaller than the error bars on returns. This result is a primary reason why risk parity strategies have gained in popularity.[4] But just how compelling is the decrease in error bars that risk parity offers? Figure 5.5 shows the risk parity portfolio with error bars, alongside a utility-maximized portfolio with similar amounts of total equity plus real estate allocation (which is a quick way to normalize away the effects of volatility on error bars reviewed in the previous paragraph). As you can see, the risk parity error bars are a fraction of the size of the error bars on a portfolio with similar levels of risk that was built from our utility maximization process. While the error bars in risk parity are indeed eye-popping, the major issue with this routine is that it is completely agnostic of client specifics, appropriate only

	$\gamma = 6, \lambda = 2, \varphi = 0$	Risk Parity
Equities - Domestic - Div. LO ARP	23% ± 9%	13% ± 1%
Real Estate - Domestic - Passive	0% ± 5%	10% ± 2%
Duration - Domestic - Passive	24% ± 14%	22% ± 3%
Commodities - Passive	7% ± 7%	14% ± 2%
Equities - Domestic - Div. l/s ARP	46% ± 18%	41% ± 4%

FIGURE 5.5 Error Bars on Utility Optimization vs. Risk Parity

---

[4]Risk parity allocations force each asset class to contribute the same amount of volatility to the portfolio.

	1972-2018	1989-2018	1999-2018	2009-2018
Equities - Domestic - Div. LO ARP	53% ± 26%	58% ± 36%	41% ± 40%	68% ± 49%
Real Estate - Domestic - Passive	0% ± 14%	0% ± 21%	12% ± 42%	3% ± 45%
Duration - Domestic - Passive	38% ± 27%	42% ± 36%	46% ± 40%	29% ± 40%
Commodities - Passive	9% ± 19%	0% ± 12%	0% ± 14%	0% ± 0%
Equities - Domestic - Div. l/s ARP	0% ± 22%	0% ± 18%	1% ± 34%	0% ± 6%

FIGURE 5.6 Error Bars on Optimization Results as a Function of Sample Size
($\gamma = 6$, $\lambda = 1$, and $\varphi = 0$)

for clients with high generalized risk aversion (as evidenced from the allocations matching a utility-optimal portfolio with loss aversion of 2), and in the environment where third and higher moments are inconsequential. Nonetheless, risk parity is an interesting case study to help us build our intuition around error bars.

Figure 5.6 shows the optimization results for a portfolio with $\gamma = 6$, $\lambda = 1$, and $\varphi = 0$ as we change the lookback history used for our outcome forecasts. As you can see, as sample size is increased, the error bars on our dominant allocations decrease, exactly the behavior we would hope for. What we are seeing is estimation error going down as the sample size increases, which is directly leading to smaller error bars on our prescribed portfolios.

Finally, Figure 5.7 explores asset allocation sensitivity due to asset redundancy by comparing our results with those of portfolios that include redundant assets. The analysis begins with the $\gamma = 6$, $\lambda = 1$, and $\varphi = 0$ portfolio with the five assets we have focused on throughout the chapter; we then proceed to add US small caps to the portfolio to analyze the effect of adding an asset significantly redundant to our core equity holding. Next, we add the 10-year Treasury asset to create a similar effect relative to our

	Original	+ US Small Cap	+ 10 Year Treasury	+ US Small Cap & 10 Year Treasury
Equities - Domestic - Div. LO ARP	53% ± 26%	53% ± 34%	49% ± 31%	49% ± 35%
Real Estate - Domestic - Passive	0% ± 14%	0% ± 16%	0% ± 18%	0% ± 13%
Duration - Domestic - Passive	38% ± 27%	38% ± 28%	12% ± 34%	12% ± 40%
Commodities - Passive	9% ± 19%	9% ± 18%	7% ± 19%	7% ± 19%
Equities - Domestic - Div. l/s ARP	0% ± 22%	0% ± 17%	0% ± 11%	0% ± 16%
US Small Cap	NA	0% ± 13%	NA	0% ± 8%
10 Year Treasury	NA	NA	32% ± 40%	32% ± 45%

FIGURE 5.7 Error Bars on Optimization Results as a Function of Asset Universe
($\gamma = 6$, $\lambda = 1$, and $\varphi = 0$)

core longer duration asset. Finally, we see the bootstrapped results for a portfolio that includes both redundant assets.[5]

In the case of adding just US small caps, we see some increase in error bars for our core equity holding, but nothing crazy. Notice, however, that this new holding we have added also is not pulling any assets away from our core allocation. So, despite our intuitive sense that US small caps would be redundant enough to compete with our core US equity asset, the optimizer is not flagging it as a compelling relative asset, helping keep the error bars low. The 10-year Treasury asset, on the other hand, introduces significantly more error into the mix due to its redundant nature relative to our longer duration asset, which is clearly being flagged by the optimizer as more interesting relative to our core duration asset. And these were just two assets picked out of a hat; if one were to create a portfolio with 30 assets, many of which were similar, we would see much more error bar chaos prevail.

FINAL REMARKS

This book has brought modern features from behavioral economics into our client's risk profile, along with a modernized system for incorporating financial goals into the asset allocation process, and has enabled incorporation of more realistic higher moment behavior into the asset allocation process. This book has also focused on creating a practical framework by enabling streamlined forecasting from history while tackling the challenges that estimation error presents by deploying statistically sound estimation techniques and avoiding redundant assets.

The goal of this book was to empower financial advisors to confidently build portfolios that are truly personalized for their clients. I hope we have indeed taken a solid step toward such a modern yet practical asset allocation framework.

---

[5]The 10-year Treasury is represented by a constant maturity index from the Center for Research in Security Prices at the University of Chicago's Booth School of Business (CRSP®). US small cap data is from Ken French's online library, where we use the bottom quintile of equities sorted on size.

Bibliography

Abdellaoui, Bleichrodt, & Paraschiv. (2007). Loss Aversion Under Prospect Theory: A Parameter-Free Measurement. *Management Science*, 1659–1674.

Adler & Kritzman. (2007). Mean-Variance versus Full-Scale Optimisation: In and Out of Sample. *Journal of Asset Management*, 302–311.

Ang. (2014). *Asset Management: A Systematic Approach to Factor Investing*. New York: Oxford University Press.

Baucells & Villasis. (2010). Stability of Risk Preferences and the Reflection Effect of Prospect Theory. *Theory & Decision*, 193–211.

Benartzi & Thaler. (1999). Risk Aversion of Myopia? Choices in Repeated Gambles and Retirement Investments. *Management Science*, 364–381.

Campbell & Cochrane. (1999). By Force of Habit: A Consumption-Based Explanation of Aggregate Stock Market Behavior. *Journal of Political Economy*, 205–251.

CFA Institute. (2018). *CFA Program Curriculum 2019 Level III*. Wiley.

Cremers, Kritzman, & Page. (2004). Optimal Hedge Fund Allocation: Do Higher Moments Matter? *Revere Street Working Paper Series, Financial Economics*, 272–313.

Donadelli & Prosperi. (2011). The Equity Risk Premium: Empirical Evidence from Emerging Markets. http://ssrn.com/abstract=1893378.

Fagley. (1993). A Note Concerning Reflection Effects Versus Framing Effects. *Psychological Bulletin*, 451–452.

Gachter, Johnson, & Herrmann. (2007). Individual-Level Loss Aversion in Riskless and Risky Choices. *Centre for Decision Research and Experimental Economics*, Paper No. 2007-02.

Grable. (2017). Financial Risk Tolerance: A Psychometric View. *CFA Institute Research Foundation: Research Foundation Briefs*.

Grable & Lytton. (1999). Financial Risk Rolerance Revisited: The Development of a Risk Assessment Instrument. *Financial Services Review*, 163–181.

Grinold. (1999). Mean-Variance and Scenario-Based Approaches to Portfolio Selection. *Journal of Portfolio Management*, 10–22.

Guillemette, Yao, & James. (2015). An Analysis of Risk Assessment Questions Based on Loss-Averse Preferences. *Journal of Financial Counseling and Planning*, 17–29.

Hamdan, Pavlowsky, Roncalli, & Zheng. (2016). A Primer on Alternative Risk Premia. https://ssrn.com/abstract=2766850, 1–123.

Holt & Laury. (2002). *Risk Aversion and Incentive Effects*. Andrew Young School of Policy Studies Research Paper Series.

Ilmanen. (2012). Expected Returns on Major Asset Classes. *Research Foundation of CFA Institute.*

Ilmanen, A. (2011). *Expected Returns: An Investor's Guide to Harvesting Market Rewards.* West Sussex: Wiley.

Kahneman & Taversky. (1979). Prospect Theory: An Analysis of Decision under Risk. *Econometrica,* 263–292.

Kinlaw, Kritzman, & Turkington. (2017). *A Practitioner's Guide to Asset Allocation.* Hoboken: Wiley.

Kraus & Litzenberger. (1976). Skewness Preferences and the Valuation of Risk Assets. *The Journal of Finance,* 1085–1100.

Lemperiere, Deremble, Nguyen, Seager, Potters, & Bouchaud. (2014). *Risk Premia: Asymmetric Tail Risks and Excess Returns.* https://papers.ssrn.com/sol3/papers .cfm?abstract_id=2502743.

Levy. (1992). An Introduction to Prospect Theory. *Political Psychology,* 171–186.

Maginn, Tuttle, Pinto, & McLeavey. (2007). *Managing Investment Portfolios: A Dynamic Process.* Hoboken: Wiley.

Markowitz. (2010). Portfolio Theory: As I Still See It. *Annual Reviews of Financial Economics,* 1–23.

Meucci, A. (n.d.). Retrieved from ARPM Lab—www.arpm.co: www.arpm.co.

Moore, Sapra, & Pedersen. (2017). *The PIMCO Glide Patch Construction Process.* PIMCO Quantitative Research.

Neuberger & Payne. (2018). The Skewness of the Stock Market at Long Horizons. *Frontiers of Factor Investing.*https://papers.ssrn.com/sol3/papers.cfm?abstract_ id=3173581.

Pompian. (2006). *Behavioral Finance and Wealth Management.* Hoboken: Wiley.

Roncalli. (2017). *Alternative Risk Premia: What Do We Know?* Retrieved from Thierry Roncalli's Home Page: http://www.thierry-roncalli.com/download/ Alternative_Risk_Premia_WDWK.pdf.

Samuelson. (1963). Risk and Uncertainty: A Fallacy of Large Numbers. *Scientia,* 108–113.

Scott & Horvath. (1980). On the Direction of Preference for Moments of Higher Order than the Variance. *The Journal of Finance,* 915–919.

Sharpe. (1964). Capital Asset Prices: A Theory of Market Equilibrium Under Conditions of Risk. *The Journal of Finance,* 425–442.

Thaler & Johnson. (1990). Gambling with the House Money and Trying to Break Even: The Effects of Prior Outcomes on Risky Choice. *Management Science,* 643–660.

Wilcox, Horvitz, & di Bartolomeo. (2006). Investment Management for Taxable Private Investors. *Research Foundation of CFA Institute.*

Wright & Herrington. (2011). Problematic Standard Errors and Confidence Intervals. *Behavioral Research,* 8–17.

Index